UNCLE JACK'S ESTATE

BY

Harry Hodson

Visit us online at www.authorsonline.co.uk

An Authors OnLine Book

Authors OnLine Ltd
40 Castle Street
Hertford SG14 1HR
England

This book is also available in e-book format, details of which are available at www.authorsonline.co.uk

This book is dedicated to the memories of Kitty, Dick, and "Uncle Jack".

ACKNOWLEDGMENTS

Also, the author feels that his younger siblings, Sylvia, Jack, Ian, and Sandra, should have some recognition. All of them having spent some of their early life with Uncle Jack, perhaps they have their own tale to tell.

ABOUT THE AUTHOR

The author is a retired engineering worker, who now spends his spare time pottering about in his garden workshop. He also finds time to write articles on all topics of the Industrial Revolution, of which a considerable number have been published at home and abroad, including contributions to television programmes. It is this interest in the past that prompted him to change course for a little while, and write about everyday life in a Lancashire Pit Village between the years 1940-60. His personal experience of spending time with his elderly neighbour has resulted in the pair of them being the central characters of the story. Uncle Jacks Estate, is the authors way of expressing the nostalgic memories of his youth, spent at a time when the world moved at a slower pace, and with different values.

PREFACE

It was not the easiest of times to be growing up in 1940's Britain, the obvious reasons being war-time conditions for half of the decade, and the post-war austerity for the remainder of the decade. However, regardless of the hardships imposed on the nation by such conditions, this period in time is now looked back upon with nostalgia and fond memories by many people.

All periods in time leave behind favourite memories for most people, but the 1940's and 50's will long remain etched in the nation's history, as an *'Extra Special Time'*. There is hardly a day goes by when the media does not inform us of this period in time; by way of a television comedy or drama, or the newspapers and magazines display articles and old black and white photographs of the way we used to live.

Of course, the media often go well beyond this period and into earlier times to remind us how we used to live. But for a generation of people who are still alive, the 1940's and 50's will always hold a special place in their hearts, because it changed the way they lived, like no other period before, or since. It was still very much part of a world that many thought had been changed by the Great War, but change came slowly for many people, especially those who lived in the industrial towns and villages of North West England.

It was still a world of Victorian terraced houses, smoking factory chimneys, collieries, coal tips, cobbled streets, gas lamps, and corner shops which displayed brightly coloured enamel signs advertising such famous names and brands as: Oxo, Marmite, Bovril, Zebo Polish, Cadburys Cocoa, Hovis, etc, etc.

'Uncle Jack's Estate' is the story of the author's own experiences of growing up in a pit village during these times, when grocers' shops had the aroma of butter, cheese, and ground coffee, and schoolrooms smelled of chalk and ink. Many of the characters are sadly no longer with us; others have made their own way through life (for good or bad), but all of them are fondly remembered by the author.

Perhaps 'Uncle Jack's Estate' will re-kindle the memory of the reader who lived through these times, or maybe provide some interest to a younger reader in search of some light-hearted reading of that period. Whatever the case may be, 'Uncle Jack's Estate' should help you indulge in a little nostalgia, and provide a little insight into the world of bygones and antiques.

EARLY DAYS

Harry Hudson was born into a working family in a mining village in the Northwest of England, one month before the outbreak of the Second World War. It was not really what you could call 'a good start in life', especially as Harry was the eldest of five children all born in quick succession in the wartime years. It was a difficult time for everyone, whatever their class and young Harry was no worse off than most of his friends and neighbours, although he sometimes thought he was.

The wartime years meant that there was a shortage of most things, so non-essentials such as toys or children's games etc. were in short supply and usually of inferior quality. When Harry used to tire of squabbling with his brothers and sisters over broken toys, torn books, and boring board games, he would go next door to 'Uncle Jack's' to look at some 'proper things'.

Uncle Jack was a retired colliery worker in his early seventies. He had retired in 1940; one year after Harry had been born, so he was more or less around all the time, apart from when he was attending to his poultry plot. Uncle Jack's house was superior to Harry's house, by the very fact it had three bedrooms; the Hudson's were cramped into a two up and two down, all seven of them. At least they could all come and go as they pleased any time of the day. At Uncle Jacks, they were always welcome.

This was a relief for Harry's mother Kitty, especially on Mondays, which was of course washday. Kitty would then pack the younger children, who were not attending school, off to Uncle Jack's, this enabled her to get on with the week's washing with the aid of two 'dolly tubs' and a coal fired boiler, taking in his washing in exchange for his childminding. This was the situation then, the Hudson's living at No. 33 and Uncle Jack Howell living at No. 31, with comings and goings between the two houses at all times of day.

Uncle Jack Howell was really no relation at all to the Hudson's, 'Uncle' or 'Aunt' was an expression you were required to use when addressing very close friends who were much older than yourself.

3

Jack Howell was known as 'John Willie' to the rest of the neighbours in the village of Hindsford.

He had lived at No. 3I Green Street since the house had been built in 1900, when the first occupant was his mother. The house was one of four that had been built by the local CO-OP; they were much larger than the rest of the houses in the same street, and normally reserved for their own employees. This was a well known fact in the village. There were also several large families who wished to get their hands on any of these houses for the increased accommodation they needed.

In reality, there was very little chance of getting one. In the first place you had to become a member of the CO-OP, then you had to wait for someone to die, and with a bit of luck if no employee required the house, you could join the waiting list. The alternative to this was to apply for a three bedroom council house out of the village; the alternative prevailed nine times out of ten.

So, how then did Uncle Jack manage to occupy one of these houses, when all his working life had been spent working in one of the local collieries?. It was a question that had been put to Uncle Jack by young Harry after the older man had told him stories of his working life in the coal mine.

"Well lad, if anyone is entitled to live in one of these here houses, then I am," said the old man." Let me tell you lad, my mother founded the CO-OP, and there would be no CO-OP without the efforts of her and a few other women."

With that, the old man climbed onto the arm rest of an easy chair and opened the doors of the built-in cupboard at the side of the chimney breast. He reached onto the top shelf and grasped a large ornamental drinking mug, stepped down, and placed the mug onto the table.

"See that" said Uncle Jack proudly, "That was made in 1886 to celebrate the opening of Hindsford CO-OP."

Harry gazed at the coloured decorative mug which bore, around its top rim, the words: THE HINDSFORD AND ATHERTON CO-OP SOCIETY FOUNDED 1886.

The mug was in pristine condition, and this interested him as he was curious to know how it had survived for so long without being broken or damaged.

'There is certainly nothing of that age in our house' he thought, 'it would have been lost or broken by other members of the family'.

4

Unknown to Harry, there *was* something in the Hudson household that was older than the CO-OP mug.

Harry then enquired why the mug was inscribed with the village name of Hindsford preceding that of Atherton; after all, Hindsford was only a village in the much larger town of Atherton.

"My mother and Mrs Carter, Mrs Bolsover and Mrs So-and-so etc, got their heads together and rented No. 43 Lord Street and that is where the CO-OP was started" said Uncle Jack.

"But it's only a house; it's where the Jones's live, I go to school with them" said Harry.

"I know that" said Uncle Jack, "but it's where the first shop used to be before they moved to the larger premises on Tyldesley Road."

With that, the old man opened a drawer below the cupboard and brought out a small booklet. "Here…look at that" he said.

On the front of the booklet were the words, 'FIFTY GLORIOUS YEARS 1886-1936'. The book contained a brief history of the Hindsford and Atherton CO-OP, from its humble beginnings to present-day activities, and now boasting more than 20 shops, with an annual turnover of £236,000.

"My mother would have been proud of that, if she were still living." said Uncle Jack.

But Harry was more interested in the good condition of the book, and wondered why things could not be looked after like that in his house. He knew that Uncle Jack had plenty of old things in the house, and he suddenly wished to know more about them.

"Can we look at some more old things?" asked Harry.

"Aye, but not now" said the old man, "it's time to tend plot and feed t' hens."

Harry went back home, to next door. He sometimes went to the plot with Uncle Jack, but he liked it best when the old man carried out repairs to the poultry sheds and fencing, this gave him a chance to go into the tool shed for a hammer, nails, and a saw. The tool shed was full of old cobwebs, rusty tools, old wooden soap boxes full of junk and bric-a-brac, and an assortment of old tins in which the nails were kept. Harry liked the old tins best; he was attracted to the decorative coloured enamel paint. Besides that, tins were strong and made to last – better than cardboard and the 'new fangled' plastic containers that were beginning to come onto the scene in the late 1940's. He would daydream in the shed, trying to get a proper look at everything, and he promised himself he would have his own tool shed when he grew up.

Harry would then be jolted back into life by a shout from Uncle Jack: "Come on lad. Let's get started, and be careful with that saw. I've had it since 1922."

The contents of Jack Howell's house were very much varied, especially when it came to their year of manufacture. For instance, the latest item was probably a 'Murphy' radio, which he had purchased in 1936. He had been influenced by Harry's father, Dick, who was a radio enthusiast and had a similar model. On the other hand, there were a few items of furniture that dated back to Victorian times, and possibly before then.

Jack Howell had been born in 1875 and much of the furniture had been left to him by his parents. There were also some pieces of furniture that were reasonably modern – 1930's style with a hint of 'Art Deco' about them. Stranger still, there were a number of artefacts that had an African origin about them; these were in the form of snakes and crocodiles etc., made from carved wood and ivory.

In later years Harry learned that the African artefacts had been brought to the house by 'Aunt Jean'. Harry could just about remember 'Aunt Jean'; she used to baby-sit him as a child and was a great help to his mother Kitty whenever another child came along. She died when Harry was six years old. Uncle Jack inherited her possessions because she lived with him, although they were not married. They called it 'living over the brush' in those days.

In later years Harry questioned Uncle Jack as to why he did not have a 'real wife', after learning Aunt Jean and him were never married.

"Well if tha must know lad, I will tell thee," said the old man.

Harry had taken a risk by asking the question, and could have been severely rebuked for it. It was a time when children were meant to he seen and not heard, but Harry was then twelve years old, and considered to be a 'man of the world' by the old man.

"My wife is alive and well. She lives in West Street with our Hannah," said Uncle Jack.

"But why did she leave you?" Harry asked.

"She didn't leave me. I told her to go…" he said.

"But why did you tell her to go?" said Harry.

"By heck lad, if tha keeps on, tha'll know as much as me" said Uncle Jack. "It were like this...I was earning four sovereigns a week in them days, but she was spending five sovereigns; fancy clothes and things. You can't do that lad, sooner or later you will get into trouble."

Harry got the message and did not pursue the matter any further. "What's a sovereign look like, Uncle Jack?"

"I'll show thee some other time, it's time to get tea started," muttered the old man.

Back in his own home, Harry waited until the evening meal had finished before putting the question of Uncle Jack's marital breakdown to his parents. His father answered loud and clear.

"John Willie is a thrifty old bugger as we all know, gets it from his mother you know. If she were still running the CO-OP it would be making even bigger profits than it already is. There was nowt much wrong with his wife, apart from her being opposite to him where money was concerned. Fetched four children up and they've all done alreet for themselves. I think it was six-of-one and half a dozen of the other between them two."

Dick Hudson was addressing not only Harry, but also his own wife Kitty, Harry's mother. Kitty was Dick's second wife and was eighteen years younger than him, so she had not been on the scene long enough to know too much of Uncle Jack's past. The eighteen year age difference between Harry's parents had a lasting effect on him and his brothers and sisters, due to their totally different ideas and personalities.

Harry was passing the time of day at Uncle Jack's when the old man said, "While you're here lad, you can give us a lift emptying this showcase, it is due for a clean-out."

It was the moment Harry had been waiting for; he had known the showcase all his life, but had never actually seen it open. It was always firmly locked, and the key was thrown into a tin containing dozens of other keys, only identifiable to their owner. The contents of the showcase could, of course, be seen through the glass panels. There was an assortment of pottery and books, and a few very old photographs.

One book in particular had fascinated young Harry all his life, it occupied centre place on the bottom shelf of the showcase. It was the largest book Harry had ever seen; or, for that matter, that anyone else in the village had ever seen. It was two feet high, and eight inches thick, leather bound with gold ornate lettering bearing the name 'HOLY BIBLE'.

"Right" said Uncle Jack, "first of all, we'll empty the pottery and put it in the middle of the table, it will be safe there."

Harry was amazed he was about to be trusted with handling the contents of the showcase...

"Be careful lad, some of that pottery has been around since before my time," said the old man.

Harry was nervous and would be glad when they got onto the books; books don't break when they are dropped. He also noticed that the pottery was in sets; like 4 cups, 4 saucers, 4 plates and so on, with matching jugs and various condiments. There was very little pottery in Harry's house that could come up to these standards; it was one of this, two of that, and the rest missing, probably broken by his younger brothers and sisters, these were his thoughts. Then he would suddenly remember there was a matching set of pottery on the second shelf of the chimney breast cupboard at home. But this was sometimes used when relatives came to Sunday tea, so it was not valuable.

"Right. That's all the pottery out." said Uncle Jack. "...hand painted some of these you know," but that meant nothing to Harry, he had his eyes set on bigger things.

There was now a fine display of pottery in the centre of the table; birds, flowers and country scenes adorned the cups, saucers, and plates, all painted in brilliant reds, yellows, greens and blues. Uncle Jack picked up a plate and ran his fingers over the petals of the flower pattern around its outer rim. "Here, you do that lad and tell me what you can feel."

Harry did the same. "I think I can feel the flowers" he said, not quite sure of himself and wondering whether it was his imagination.

"Of course you can," said Uncle Jack, "it's the thickness of the paint; nowadays it's nearly always put on by transfers."

Harry did not want to become involved in a lecture about transfers, he already knew what they were, you sometimes got them free with the weekly comic and you and your pals stuck them on each other's forearm.

"Put all the books around the edge of the table" said Uncle Jack, as he started to lift them out of the showcase.

Harry did as he was told, occasionally flicking through the pages of a few of them, but most of them did not have pictures, so he was not interested. There were now only two books left in the showcase. One was the Great 'HOLY BIBLE', still occupying centre place on the bottom shelf. It remained in its place as Uncle Jack carefully placed his hands around the second book and lifted it out onto the table.

This book was easily the next largest book in the showcase, but even so it was only half the size of the Great Bible. This book was unlike anything that Harry had ever seen; its leather bound covers were held together by gold plated metal straps which clasped together to keep the book closed. Uncle Jack unfastened the clasps and opened the book.

"It's called 'Pilgrims Progress'" said the old man as he thumbed through the pages, occasionally stopping to view the fine coloured plates. "Everyone should read 'Pilgrims Progress', and maybe we would have a much better world than we have now," he continued as he closed and fastened the book.

The bright lettering – done in copperplate between the metal straps of the book, bore the title 'Pilgrims Progress by John Bunyan'.

"Is that real gold?" said Harry, pointing to the lettering.

"Well, I suppose it is," said Uncle Jack, "but it's what they call gold leaf; gold is very rare and expensive, so there is only a tiny amount in this lettering."

Harry had a fascination with gold and wished to see a proper piece of it, something like a coin would do, something like you see in the pirates' treasure chests in a story book. He was tired of adults who told him to look at his mother's wedding ring. With 'Pilgrims Progress' firmly closed and put back on the table, the great moment had arrived for Harry. It was time to lift the great book out of the showcase.

"I think we will leave the Holy Bible where it is and dust around it." Uncle Jack stated.

The words echoed and re-echoed in Harry's ears; he was dumbstruck. He quickly recovered and gathered his senses about him. He was not going to wait all his life to look inside the 'Great Book' and be cheated out of it at this stage. He had a very good memory, and quickly recalled something he had heard at school some time ago.

"Uncle Jack – can you remember when I told you that the school teacher said there was no such thing as the Devil?" he quickly blurted out. "Miss Barrow said the Devil is a mythical creature that has been dreamed up to frighten us from doing wrong, and if we were properly brought up, then we would do no wrong. You told me this was rubbish, and there *is* a Devil, and one day you would show me what he looks like, and we can see him in the Great Bible.

Uncle Jack was cornered. "So I did lad, so I did," said the old man as he stooped down to lift the Great book from its resting place. "What do Ethel and Elsie Barrow know?" he muttered as he gently eased the book from out of the showcase.

Ethel and Elsie Barrow were two spinster sisters in their fifties who had taught at the school all their working lives. "I remember them starting to teach forty odd years ago, seems they've not learned much themselves," said Uncle Jack as he lay the book flat on the floor.

"Now then lad, give us a lift onto the table with this book, it's very heavy you know."

The book was indeed very heavy, but could probably be lifted by one person alone; it was Uncle Jack's way of creating an impression on Harry, of the importance of the Great Book. The two of them lifted the book onto the table. At long last Harry's great moment had come.

Uncle Jack opened it to a section he was familiar with and started to turn the pages. Harry noticed the heading at the top of the pages, '*The Temptation of Christ in the Wilderness*'. All of a sudden the pages stopped turning at a large coloured lithograph.

"Here, look at this," said Uncle Jack.

Harry was shocked by what he saw; a cold shiver ran through his body. This was the kind of feeling you only read about in story books.

The scene was one of semi-desert, with a few sparse plants struggling for survival. All around were weird fictitious creatures with large popping eyes, their faces twisted with pain and misery. The Devil himself occupied the foreground, in the centre of the picture. He was in the form of a huge animal, very much like an Australian kangaroo. His body was covered in very stiff brown hair; his hands and feet were cloven, and his ears and tail were pointed. He was stood on his hind legs like a human being and he held a large trident in one arm and a burning torch in the other. The look on his face would strike fear into the souls of the hardest of people. Two large green eyes popped out from his twisted face, and he appeared to be scowling and grinning at the same time. If this was meant to shock, then it had clearly succeeded in Harry's case. It was a very fine example of the great skills of the artist and lithographer who had created the scene.

Depressing thoughts began to overtake Harry, and he was beginning to wish he had never seen the picture. He gathered his thoughts together and tried to reassure himself that it was only a picture, yet one part of his mind kept telling him that such horrible scenes must have existed in past times; and pain and misery were suffered by *real* people. He looked up and saw Uncle Jack with a stern look upon his face.

The old man spoke first. "Owt about thers no Devil, you've seen him for yourself, and this book tells no lies." Uncle Jack's words had such chilling tones that Harry wished he had never become involved in the situation.

There were a few moments silence as the two looked at each other; it seemed an eternity to Harry, but it was the old man's way of getting home the message of right and wrong. Uncle Jack closed the Great Book and went into the kitchen as Harry recovered from his experience. He came back from the kitchen with a bowl of lukewarm water and some 'gentle' soap flakes and two cloths.

He swirled a few of the soap flakes around in the bowl and dropped some of the pottery into it. "Right lad, you wash the pots and I will dry them and put them back into the showcase."

"But they're not dirty," said Harry.

"We've taken the trouble of getting them out so we'll put them back in a proper state," the old man added.

With the pottery cleaned, the books dusted and put back into the showcase, Uncle Jack reached for the key and firmly locked it.

"There. I reckon that's a good morning's work," he muttered satisfactorily, "I think its time for dinner."

That same evening, Harry was not looking forward to going to bed. He was afraid he might have dreams in which he would see the Devil. His father sat in front of the coal fire reading the evening paper whilst his mother bathed the younger children in a tin bath on the rug near the hearthstone. Now was a good time to confide in them both at the same time.

He told them his fears of what he had seen in the Great Bible in Uncle Jack's house. His father laughed out loudly but his mother remained silent, with a slightly troubled look upon her face. She had a great respect for Uncle Jack and considered him to be a reasonably educated man who was usually correct in what he said. Harry's father was more or less in agreement with Miss Barrow the teacher, and reassured him there was nothing to fear if you did nothing wrong. Harry felt a little more confident; after all, no harm had befallen his mother and father, so all he had to do was to lead his life by their example. He started to cheer up, especially when his mother said he could stay up another hour and read his comics or listen to 'Radio Luxemburg' as it was the school holidays and there was no need to get up early.

SCHOOL TIME

Harry came home from school one afternoon and spoke to his mother: "Miss Barrow says could we all bring a plate, cup, saucer, a spoon, knife and fork."

"It's not party time yet," said his mother, Kitty. "You don't normally have a party until Christmas time."

That was quite true, but there had been one occasion, Harry remembered, it had happened before.

"That must have been V. J. Day, so what is it this time?" said Kitty.

"Miss Barrow says the whole country needs cheering up and now there is a good reason to do so," said Harry.

It was a dull, damp November day in 1947, and the country had just been informed of the forthcoming marriage of H.R.H. Princess Elizabeth, to Prince Phillip of Greece.

"I think I know what it is now," said Kitty "It is Princess Elizabeth's wedding.''

Miss Barrow and the other teachers had taken it upon themselves to celebrate the occasion, with the whole school listening to a radio broadcast in the morning, followed by a little tea party in the afternoon.

On the day of the wedding, the whole school was packed into the main hall, and an ancient old radio was coupled to the loud-speakers. At 11 AM, the radio was tuned into the BBC by the school caretaker. It crackled away as the plum-voiced announcer began to describe the events.

The six female spinster teachers listened intently as the events of the wedding unfolded, occasionally dabbing the moisture from their eyes. Watching over them from a seat behind was the headmaster, Mr Bardsley.

Reginald Stanley Bardsley was a more than sufficient deterrent to guarantee absolute silence and good behaviour from the pupils on occasions like this. He was six feet and three inches tall, and aged about sixty. He was now in the process of grooming one of the younger female teachers to take his place when he retired, as he had been headmaster since 1921. In fact, he was only the second person to have held the post since the school had opened in 1874.

The previous occupant had been an ex Indian Army Officer, James C. Carruthers. Mr Bardsley had inherited the ex army officer's strict Victorian disciplinary principles needed to deal with unruly pupils. He had never married and this had been cause for tittle-tattle amongst some of the older pupils, regarding his affections for the female staff. Some parents were concerned that the position of head teacher should not be handed to a female. They believed they would not be able to control some of the older pupils. However, the education act of 1944 stated that pupils over the age of eleven years could no longer be taught at the school and unless they qualified for Grammar School, they would have to attend one of the large Senior Schools out of the village. This explained why the position was open to female staff.

The natural choice was Harry's teacher, Miss Barrow. Ethel Barrow was a few years younger than her sister Elsie. She was the stronger of the two, although Elsie taught the senior class. Much of the tittle-tattle over the years had been focussed on the liaison between Ethel and Mr Bardsley, so it was assumed she would be his natural successor.

With mid-day approaching, the events of the Royal Wedding began to wind down and the pupils were looking forward to their lunch break of one and a half hours. At twelve noon the radio was switched off and the school was dismissed for 'dinner break', this being the term used when referring to your mid-day meal in North West England. Most of the pupils made their way home for lunch; whilst a few stayed on to partake in the newly-introduced school meals scheme.

Harry made his way home with his younger brother and sister. Like most of the pupils, they only lived a couple of minutes walk from the school. Kitty had spent the morning doing housework and looking after the two youngest children, who were not yet school age. Two sets of plain white pottery with knives forks and spoons were packed into a shopping basket on the table.

"Where's mine?" said Harry.

Kitty lifted a thick brown paper bag into the basket. "They're in here. But be careful with them. I don't know what your dad will say if he knows about this," she said.

Back at school that afternoon, each child was told to lay out their cup, saucer, spoon etc., on top of their desk. If the desk lid sloped, they were told to pack it with books until it was level. Harry's class had been informed there would be a lesson beforehand, and the tea party would be from two-thirty until home time at four. The news of the lesson was greeted with dismay by some of the pupils, but Harry didn't mind because it was his favourite subject – history.

Miss Barrow wrote a few questions on the blackboard and began to move up and down the classroom between the rows of desks.

"The Romans did indeed have hot and cold running water," she shouted in loud clear tones. She was answering one of the 'better off' children who lived in one of the pre-war semi-detached houses on the outskirts of the village. "These houses were equipped with hot running water and bathrooms, and were the only ones in the village with such facilities."

Thirty-odd hands were thrust into the air with cries of "But Miss Barrow, we have not got hot water."

"I know, I know…but things will change," she said.

She immediately strode over to Harry's desk. He was half expecting her to ask him a question on the Romans, but the question never came.

"Good Heavens! Does your mother know you have brought these here?" she cried as she lifted up each piece of pottery from on top of the desk.

"Yes Miss. She gave them to me," said Harry as Miss Barrow began to admire the ornate decorative patterns of green, red, and gold. Some of the class began to stand up in an effort to get a better look at the pottery on Harry's desk, after all, some of them had brought coloured pottery and Miss Barrow had walked past it without so much as a glance.

Just then, the silence of the moment was broken by the classroom door being opened; in walked Miss Smeaton, teacher of 'standard one' class. She had come to enquire if everyone was ready to start the party in a few minutes time.

"Will you come and have a look at these?" said Miss Barrow, as she held a cup and saucer in her hands.

The two of them reached into their heavy woollen cardigan pockets and put on their spectacles, for a closer examination.

15

"I think it is of Japanese origin, according to the maker's mark." Miss Barrow stated.

"Sounds like it, by the name 'Noritakee'," said Miss Smeaton as she picked up a plate to view the manufacturer's mark.

Miss Smeaton was younger than Miss Barrow by quite a few years. She looked up to her, and often sought her advice on various matters. Nevertheless, she seemed to be playing a far more important role in the day-to-day running of the school as the ageing Mr Bardsley went into semi-retirement.

It had often been commented on that there appeared to be no 'standard two' class. 'Standard one' class was taught by Miss Smeaton, 'standard three' class by Miss Ethel Barrow, and 'standard four' by Miss Elsie Barrow. Beyond 'standard four' you left the school to attend senior school. Three more female teachers controlled the infants' section of the school, the eldest of these was given the title of headmistress, but in fact they were all under the control of Mr Bardsley.

Harry had done his first year term in junior school in Miss Smeaton's 'standard one' class; he then went from there to Ethel Barrow's 'standard three' class, yet some of his friends went upstairs to be taught by Mr Bardsley. This was a funny situation. The class was much smaller than the other classes, and there appeared to be no 'standard two' on the classroom door.

Harry, and others like him, thought they had gained instant promotion in by-passing 'standard two'. In reality, Mr Bardsley had hand-picked some of the brighter pupils, and off-loaded the rest onto Ethel Barrow at 'standard three', thereby forcing her to teach on two different levels in the same classroom.

The two teachers placed the pottery back on Harry's desk and told him to be very careful with it.

"It is really far too good for a tea party," said Miss Barrow.

Harry felt very proud; his life had been very insignificant up until this moment. He felt a warm glow come over him as the other pupils cast glances of admiration at the display of pottery on his desk.

"Right," said Miss Barrow, "we'll start the party..." One of the dinner ladies wheeled a trolley laden with two large metal teapots and some jugs of milk and mineral water into the classroom.

It was the usual setting; a hot pasty which always tasted delicious, three or four little sandwiches, the fillings being potted beef or cheese, ham if you were very lucky, and in the rarest of cases, salmon. This was followed by a small trifle in a wax-lined container, a few biscuits, and a piece of Victoria sponge cake, usually baked by one of the pupils' mothers; this was washed down by a cup of lukewarm tea or mineral water. Nevertheless, it was not an official celebration and some schools let the occasion pass by without recognition, therefore it was a great credit to Harry's teachers for their efforts.

He went home from school that afternoon feeling quite pleased with himself and told his mother of the incident with the pottery. Kitty rinsed and dried the pots and placed them back on the second shelf of the cupboard. "Don't tell your father I've let you use these," she remarked.

HARRY GETS A JOB

When he was not at school or helping Uncle Jack on the plot, Harry liked nothing better than to be playing outdoors with his friends.

Although these were the austere years of the 1940's, life seemed to be one long magical adventure and the sun was always shining. The dark winter nights were spent playing at the street corner under the light of the gas lamp, or in friends' houses exchanging comics or cigarette cards. Harry was very keen to own a full set of cigarette cards, but this was beyond his wildest dreams; the reason being they were no longer issued – except for one particular brand.

In pre-war days, nearly all brands of cigarettes included one card with every ten-pack purchased. Usually in sets of fifty, the cards covered hundreds of subjects such as, locomotives, ships, planes, cars, gardening hints, sporting heroes, film stars, etc. Economic wartime measures had stopped the practice, so they began to get very scarce. However, one particular brand called 'Turf', still included one of the much sought after cards with every ten-pack purchased. The down-side to this though, was that 'Turf' were not too high on the popularity list among the thousands of smokers of that period in time. Even so, they were considered to be a reasonable substitute when the leading brands were scarce due to rationing and well above dozens of others who had attracted unmentionable additions to their brand names, because of their poor quality.

By this time Harry had managed to get himself a job to earn some spending money, which was in *very* short supply in his own household. The job entailed running errands for one of the neighbours – Mrs Timperley. Mrs Timperley had a large family which consisted of a few unmarried sons who still lived with her. They were mature men in their thirties and forties; all of them smoked and drank. Her husband had left her in the depression years of the early thirties, unable to cope with the stress and strain of trying to feed and care for their large brood. Fortunately for Mrs Timperley, her two eldest sons had just started work and this eased the situation.

By the time Harry had started to run her errands in the late 1940's, she had four sons all working in the local collieries, so there was a considerable amount of income coming into the Timperley household. In view of this, it would seem the family should be reasonably prosperous; in reality it was far from it.

Mrs Timperley had very little control over any of her sons' weekly wages. They would give her just enough to buy meals and pay the rent, with little or nothing left over for life's little luxuries. The house was sparsely furnished with the cheapest type of plywood furniture which was prevalent amongst the working classes. Apart from a pendulum clock which hung on the living room wall, a rocking chair and a large Victorian sideboard, there was little else of any value in the Timperley household.

Harry used to start the errands immediately after school at 4 PM in the afternoon, and sometimes would not finish until 6 PM in the evening. This period of two hours often interrupted playing out with his pals and he sometimes wished he did not have to do the job; but the payment of one shilling and threepence per week came in very handy.

The shopping list he was given usually consisted of bread, milk, potatoes, vegetables, cooked meat, a few cakes etc. and cigarettes. These then, were everyday items, and there should have been no problems, but the cigarettes could be a problem for Harry and add a considerable amount of time to his job – with no extra pay. The first port of call would usually be the local outdoor licence-cum grocery shop, where Harry would ask for two items on his list, such as bread and milk. The shop could very likely have supplied all the articles on his list, but this did not fit into his plans. After purchasing the bread and milk, he would then look at his list again, and innocently ask for a ten-pack of the leading brand of cigarettes. With a bit of luck, the shopkeeper would then fumble underneath the counter and produce a ten-pack of the leading brand, with a sour look upon his face, muttering, "Don't you know there's rationing still on?"

Harry would then be troubled with afterthoughts. What if he had purchased all the grocery items at one go? Perhaps the shopkeeper might have supplied him with twenty, or maybe forty of the leading brand in recognition of the trade in groceries; this would have saved him a lot of time and trouble with no need to visit other shops, thereby finishing his errands early.

It was a risk he could not take. If he had purchased all the items on his list at one shop, there was the possibility that the shopkeeper would still have only supplied one ten-pack of the leading brand and maybe another two ten-packs of a lesser quality brand. If this situation happened, he would have no more groceries to purchase and could therefore not go to another shop and ask for a packet of the leading brand of cigarettes without making a purchase of other goods. With the exception of newsagents, most shops would not supply you with a packet of quality cigarettes if you did not spend a certain amount of money on other goods. Incidentally, there seemed to be no legal age limit on a person wishing to purchase cigarettes in those days; if there was, then it was very rarely put into practice.

Harry would then run to his next port of call clutching a large leatherette shopping bag laden with three bottles of milk and two loaves. The next shops on his list would be another outdoor licence-cum grocery or the CO-OP. He would try to avoid the CO-OP if possible; it was usually full of old ladies wearing shawls. It was a kind of meeting place for them to pass the time of day with each other whilst making their purchases and Harry knew you could spend the best part of forty five minutes here before being served.

The routine was the same and with a bit of luck he would secure another ten-pack of the leading brand; his prime goal was to obtain forty cigarettes of the same brand, to satisfy the needs of the Timperley brothers. At this stage Harry was faced with a dilemma: he had the choice of completing his shopping list of groceries in one go, with a guaranteed twenty leading brand cigarettes and another twenty of a less popular brand. He was beginning to learn from experience that he could get away with this situation – after all, it was a compromise: twenty good and twenty not quite so good, and Mrs Timperley would share them out accordingly among her sons. The alternative was a further trip to another shop to practice the same routine, with no guaranteed result of obtaining the magical forty.

When asked what kind of cigarettes were required in the absence of the leading brand, Harry's answer was always 'Turf', even though the shopkeeper had read out a long list of comparable brands. Sometimes Harry would be present when Mrs Timperley was dishing the cigarettes out. There would be constant arguments regarding whose turn it was for the leading brand. The ideal situation would have been to share each of the different brands out.

When the arguments got out of hand, Mrs Timperley would reach into her apron pocket and produce a list of her sons' names, and what particular brand each had received during the last few days.

Sometimes this information would be challenged to be incorrect, and she would be told favouritism was taking place. She would then point out that her list was in correct rotation of fairness, because it had been made with information from Harry and he had a very good memory.

She would then reach for her walking stick and strike several swift blows on the dining table shouting, "I'll show you who is the boss in this house!"

At this stage the brothers knew they had gone far enough; they respected their mother. They would retreat to their armchairs with a pot of tea and their quota of cigarettes and eventually go to sleep.

On occasion, the brothers would question Harry as to why he always purchased 'Turf' as a standby, when there were several other brands available equally as good. Further still, their mother was always asking them to save their empty packets of 'Turf'.

One day, one of the brothers rounded on Harry just as he was about to start his errands. "Don't bring me any of those 'Turf' this time you young bugger!" he shouted.

"But it's your turn," said Harry.

"I know it is, but you can do better than that; there's so-and-so, and so-and-so. I know what your game is!" screamed Peter Timperley.

The game was up. Harry's plans were rumbled. He had been at a disadvantage by the very fact that the collectors card in every ten-pack of 'Turf', was actually part of the packet. This was the manufacturers way of getting around the strict wartime measures still in force, preventing unnecessary use of materials. In pre-war days the cards were separate and could be removed from the packet immediately on opening. The packet could then be thrown away when empty, without the trouble of cutting away a card.

At Harry's request, Mrs Timperley would sometimes remove 'Turf' cigarettes from the packet and cut out the card for him, just in case it became empty whilst no longer in the house and was thrown into the gutter.

The Timperley brothers told Harry that he was not to bring 'Turf' into the house any more; "Things are getting better and there are some good cigs about today. So shape yourself – or else!"

Harry had a good idea what the 'or else' meant; sometimes they would give him as much as a shilling bonus on top of the one shilling and threepence that Mrs Timperley gave him, especially if they were in high spirits after drink, or had a good win on the horses.

After this warning, Harry took stock of his collection of 'Turf' cards. Twenty five... and six 'twicers'. Forty were needed for a full set. The 'twicers' could of course be exchanged amongst his pals and this would get him to thirty one.

Harry began bartering with his pals to exchange the 'twicers'... he found this very difficult, especially when some boys showed him full sets of pre-war cards, some of them with fifty in a set – and all done in colour!

"Lucky devils" he would mutter, and wonder why his parents, who were both smokers, had not bothered to save the cards in pre-war days.

He was further disappointed when his pals told him that, even if he *did* have a full set of 'Turf' cards, it was nothing special. The cards were printed in one colour only – a drab kind of blue and in a series of forty, whereas most of the pre-war cards were printed in different colours and were much more popular.

Harry was now growing up very fast. He began to realise it was a tough old world that could fill you with disappointment; things did not come easily. You had to work *very* hard or be very smart or a member of a rich family. The latter could be ruled out in his case.

HAPPY DAYS

In 1940's Britain, entertainment for the working classes usually consisted of listening to the radio, or a visit to the cinema and an occasional visit to the seaside by train or 'charabanc' (motor coach). After school hours, most children entertained themselves by playing games, or with outdoor activities – depending on the weather and season.

In the spring and summer months the activities available were: football, cricket, marbles, kite-flying, top and whip, hopscotch etc. Children went for long walks in the countryside and spent hours exploring ponds and streams, having picnics of sandwiches and a bottle of water (mineral water if you were lucky).

The autumn months were spent gathering horse-chestnuts, drying them out until they became very hard, and then playing 'conkers' with them. Halloween and Bonfire Night were also great favourites, and many weeks were usually spent gathering fuel in preparation for Bonfire Night.

This was followed by the run-up to Christmas; a home-made toboggan to ride through the snow, or carol-singing, listening to the radio, or swapping comics and cigarette cards in front of a warm fire indoors. These are just a few of the activities that children of the 1940's indulged in.

Like most children of his age, Harry Hudson enjoyed this period in his life. When summer came, it seemed to go on for ever and life was one magical long adventure. The gathering of fuel for the bonfire to celebrate Guy Fawkes' night was one of Harry's favourite times. He also learned that much of the nation's good furniture was consumed on bonfires in the immediate post-war years.

From 1946 onwards, it seemed as though the whole country was throwing out its past and beginning a new way of life. Children in those days started to collect bonfire fuel from September onwards – the two week school break was a good opportunity to gather old timber and build it into a large stack. A hut was usually made from the better pieces of timber, the stack was then piled up around it.

The hut was a 'den' which offered shelter from the weather in the weeks leading up to Bonfire Night on November 5th.

Each night a small fire would be lit in front of the 'den' entrance. It gave warmth, light, and comfort to the occupants inside. The purpose of the 'den' was to guard against marauding gangs of other children who would come to steal timber for their own cause if the stack was left unguarded.

This worked both ways between rival gangs whilst their bonfires were being built. Timber came from all sources, especially old houses that were being demolished in the wake of the post-war house building programme. Children spent their after-school hours gathering anything vaguely combustible. They would even travel miles into the countryside to chop an old tree down, or carry an old railway sleeper off to add to the stack.

Householders saw it as an opportunity to get rid of their old furniture and bring in the 'new look' by purchasing new, post-war furniture. They may well have been throwing better furniture *onto* the bonfire than they were actually buying new! The reason for this: people simply wanted a change of scene. Many families still lived with their parents in rented accommodation in post-war Britain, eagerly awaiting a council house or saving for a deposit on a house of their own.

Two World Wars and the severe depression of the thirties had left many working class families with little opportunity to buy new furniture, consequently there was plenty of Edwardian and Victorian furniture still in everyday use in most homes. In later years, Harry Hudson would often recall his memories of the times he helped to throw antique furniture onto the flames of the bonfire on Guy Fawkes' night.

Harry and his pals would often be called to a house whose occupants wished to dispose of some household goods onto the bonfire. More often than not, it was usually a chest of drawers or an old sideboard that the owner wished to get rid of. Harry and his friends would enter the house and be shown the condemned piece of furniture – which was usually too big and too heavy to move. They would then set about taking out the drawers and removing various screws to split the carcass in half. If the latter did not work, then what may have been a very fine piece of antique furniture would be butchered on the spot with an axe, regardless of its fine carving or walnut veneer.

Harry would often be told off by his peers for spending time admiring the workmanship of the condemned piece. He often wished he could prevent its destruction, but dare not say so for fear of being ridiculed. Other items thrown onto the bonfire included old settees, bamboo furniture, odd chairs, bedroom furniture, old mirrors, and even Vienna Regulators. Many items, such as the last two described, would not be much use as combustible fuel, but the bonfire was an opportunity to get rid of them.

Vienna Regulators were popular from the 1880's until the middle of the 20th century. They were probably introduced as a cheaper alternative to the longcase Grandfather Clock which was becoming less fashionable. These wall-mounted clocks were usually 3-4 feet in length. A mahogany glass-fronted case housed the spring movement and porcelain dial, and the full movement of the pendulum could be seen through the glass front. Sometimes there was very little wrong with these clocks, but their owners had tired of them. Besides that, Northern working class folk could hardly afford the services of a clock repairer, so onto the bonfire they went. The flames of the fire never managed to consume the entire clock, because Harry and his pals would remove and dismantle the mechanism, share out the finely cut brass gears and spend hours spinning them like gyroscopes on a flat surface.

Settees and chairs were usually put to use for several weeks before Bonfire Night, by providing something to sit on in the 'den'. 'Settee' was thought to he a 'posh' word to describe a simple piece of furniture for sitting on. A headrest at one end allowed it to be used as a bed if required. More often than not, it was called a sofa, or couch in North-West England. Harry often remembered sitting on an old settee in the 'den' and always feeling itchy afterwards.

"I think we should get rid of it, it's full of fleas," said one of his friends. "My dad says they are filled with horsehair and are always full of fleas and there is an old couch at my Gran's we can have if we want it."

"They are not called sofa, or couch, or settee," said another boy, "They are called 'chaise longue'."

"We will have none of your fancy talk here," said an older boy, "If I say it is a *couch*, then it is a couch, and that is the end of the matter!"

Even to this day, Harry is still puzzled why such a simple piece of furniture could have four different names.

The chairs thrown onto bonfires in the immediate post-war years were usually odd chairs, some of them dating back to Victorian times; they were called 'balloon backs'. Since then, they have become collectors items and are now quite valuable. No one seemed to have the foresight to save this type of furniture in industrial North-West England. There was very little antique culture among the working classes; antiques were for 'well-to-do' folk.

Twenty years later, things had changed – thanks to TV programmes and books etc. Many working class people developed a culture for antiques. Of course, there has always been the exception; there were some wealthy families living in fine houses alongside the working classes. They had always had fine collections of antiques, but their culture did not spread to the working classes until recent years.

In present times we often hear from our friends and neighbours when they have seen a television programme, or read a book about antiques, "My old aunt had one of those and we threw it away when she died," is usually followed by: "I wish I knew then, what I know now."

Harry Hudson still echoes these words everyday, when re-calling his earlier days.

Another favourite hobby in the late forties and early fifties was recording the names and numbers of locomotives which, of course, were steam driven. Steam locomotives held a fascination for small boys and even more so, their fathers. Harry Hudson was introduced to this interesting hobby by some of the older boys.

In the first instance, you needed to buy a book which listed the names and numbers of all the locomotives in main line use in Great Britain. The book divided the locomotives into about six different categories, with their names and numbers listed below. Famous locomotives, such as the 'FLYING SCOTSMAN' and 'ROYAL SCOT' could be seen in photographs in the book, whose readers often wondered whether they would ever see them in real life.

The object of the hobby was for the owner of the book to underline the name or number of any locomotive they had seen. Some locomotives had a name and a number, but others were nameless, therefore you could only record the number. These 'locos' were less popular than the 'namers', but nevertheless they formed a very large part of the rolling stock of Britain's railways in post-war years.

Harry Hudson joined the ranks of train-spotters after he had purchased an 'Ian Allan' book. There were other books on the subject, but this was considered to be the best. Harry's book cost him one shilling and threepence (about six new pence in today's terms). He could not really afford it because it represented a full week's pay for doing Mrs Timperley's errands. He took a gamble and made the purchase on the off-chance of getting a weekend tip from one of the Timperley brothers. He was lucky that particular week. Peter Timperley gave him a silver sixpence because he had managed to get him an extra ten-pack of his favourite brand of cigarettes.

The favourite hunting grounds for Harry and his pals to do their train-spotting, were two local branch lines which had been set up by rival companies in the 19th century. One of them was the L.N.W.R. and the other was the L.Y.R.C. (London North Western and Lancashire and Yorkshire Railway Companies). Both lines were very popular with train-spotters and Harry's friends would often go there after school hours.

Harry's problem was that he was required to do Mrs Timperley's errands between the hours of 4 pm and 6 pm. This caused him a great deal of frustration, especially when his friends told him the twenty past four 'namer' had been a rare 'Jub' – (Jubilee class locomotive), which had never been seen in that part of the country before. This type of loco seemed to be the most popular with train-spotters, perhaps it was because they were the largest group of named locomotives. Many of them were named after the foreign colonial territories of Great Britain; some bore the names of Greek Gods and mythology, others had names of great generals and admirals etc.. Many of these locos worked on their own territory in various parts of the country, consequently they were seen quite often by train-spotters in that area. This led to a situation were the loco was known as a 'stinker'. Sometimes, for whatever reason, a locomotive could venture out from its normal run by two or three hundred miles, therefore it was seen by some train-spotters for the first time and declared a 'rarery' (rare). Of course, there was always the chance someone would underline the name of a rare locomotive listed in their spotters book, just to impress their friends; but no self-respecting train-spotter would resort to this, because there would be no real satisfaction in it.

Harry would often gaze at his spotters book and daydream of seeing some of the great locomotives whose wonderful sounding names had an effect on him. His greatest wish was to see TANGANYIKA, UGANDA, ZANZIBAR, AGAMEMNON, ORION and CYCLOPS – all unseen and unheard of in his part of the country. It was a vice-versa situation. These so-called 'stinkers' would be rare and unseen in other parts of the country too. It soon dawned on him that you had to travel if you wished to see rare locos.

"What's all that talking going on at the back row?" shouted Miss Barrow during an English lesson one afternoon.

"Please Miss, it's something Norman Parkinson has told us and we think everyone should know…" was the response.

"And what may that be?…quickly now, I don't want any time wasting."

One boy quickly stood up, and began to speak for the rest of them. "Norman Parkinson says his dad has told him that a very famous train will be going through Tyldesley and Atherton in two weeks time. It will pass non-stop through Tyldesley station on the L.N.W.R. line and join the L.Y.R.C. line at Atherton."

"And what will this famous train be?" Miss Barrow asked.

"It will be the 'FLYING SCOTSMAN'," shouted the rest of the class.

"The 'Flying Scotsman' indeed," said Miss Barrow, "Are you sure? It's a very important train to be coming to these parts of the country. How does Norman Parkinson know about this?" She went on.

Norman Parkinson could not readily answer, he was in a class lower than hers, being taught by Miss Smeaton in another part of the school.

Miss Barrow opened the classroom door and said: "We will soon get to know," as she made her way to Miss Smeaton's class.

She was back in a few minutes. ".Alright, alright … settle down!"

She had learned that Norman Parkinson's dad was a porter at Tyldesley Railway Station and there was some truth in the story.

"There is a possibility it may not be the 'Flying Scotsman'." She said, amidst a few groans of disappointment from the rest of the class. "However, it will be a train of equal importance. Now that is the end of the matter. Get back to your work."

It was the most talked about subject among the pupils at school in the following days. In fact, even adults were showing interest in the possibility of a famous train passing through the area. Harry Hudson was used to disappointment in his life, and did not build up his hopes that it would be the '*Flying Scotsman*'. Harry was looking forward to the event, but there were problems he would have to overcome first.

The train was due to pass through Tyldesley Station at 3.55 PM on a Tuesday; this meant everyone would still be in school. Not only that, Harry would have to do Mrs Timperley's errands between the hours of 4 and 6 PM. These problems were a cause for concern. There would not be sufficient time to get from school to the cinder embankment at Millers Lane Bridge, the best place to see the passing train. Millers Lane Bridge was about a mile from Tyldesley Station, so the train would reach there by 3.56 PM. Harry knew this would not be so much of a problem with two or three of his friends, they would simply play truant rather than miss out on this event and this frustrated him even more. It was out of the question in his case; his parents were very strict regarding school attendance, and the thought of punishment from his father was sufficient deterrent ...problems, problems.

As the days passed by, the forthcoming event became common knowledge, and there were moves afoot to make arrangements in order to witness the famous train passing through the area. There were unconfirmed reports that some schools would be let out early ensuring their pupils would not miss the event. In the wake of all this, two boys approached Miss Barrow and asked if it would be possible for school to be dismissed about twenty minutes early; this would give them time to get to the cinder embankment.

She smiled and said, "We will have to see what Mr Bardsley says. I will put the matter to him."

Reginald Stanley Bardsley was fast approaching retirement and although a strict disciplinarian, he seemed to be mellowing. But he was no-one's fool.

Two days later, after morning assembly for prayers in the school hall, he made an announcement: "I have decided to dismiss school twenty minutes early on Tuesday afternoon the 23rd of September, so you may all have a chance to see what may well be the '*Flying*

Scotsman'. Those of you who are interested, go to the cinder embankment; but keep off the track. Those who are not interested, go straight home, but in all cases you *must* inform your parents."

There were loud cheers from everyone, the pupils could not believe their luck. It seemed as though there was still something of a 'small boy' in old Bardsley, but he was no fool and saw this as a golden opportunity to guarantee absolutely perfect behaviour for the next few days. When the cheers had died down, he spoke again.

"However, I must remind you that if any pupil steps out of line or misbehaves themselves, then the privilege will be withdrawn for everybody."

There was almost perfect behaviour in the following days. Each pupil carefully watching the others and doing their utmost to produce their best work. The days passed slowly until the 23rd of September, and when the day finally arrived, Harry Hudson had already decided that Mrs Timperley's errands would have to take second place against the possibility of seeing the '*Flying Scotsman*'. He was well aware he could get into trouble by turning up late for the errands, especially if he failed to get the Timperley brothers' favourite brand of cigarettes. They would almost certainly blame it on his train-spotting and this would result in them withdrawing his tips for a while. But he had made his mind up and it was a risk he was prepared to take.

At 3.40 PM on Tuesday the 23rd of September, the school was dismissed and each teacher gave their permission for pupils to leave the classroom and make their way home. Harry and his friends made their way to the cinder embankment at Millers Lane Bridge. When they got there it was still only 3.50 PM, so there were still six minutes to choose a good position to see the passing train. Harry was amazed to see dozens of other people there, some of them were girls whom he thought would not be interested in such things. There were also older schoolboys and even adults. He scrambled up the embankment, scratching his arms and legs on bramble bushes, his shoes filled with small cinders and he was very uncomfortable, but he knew it would be worth it in the end. He found a suitable place about twelve feet from the edge of the track and decided to stay there.

Some older people were quite close to the track and this worried him a little, he had heard tales that fast moving trains could suck you onto the track if you got too close.

It was a golden autumn afternoon and the sun was still high in the sky, but suddenly, a hushed silence descended on the embankment; even the birds had stopped singing. An older boy moved quite close to the track and peered through some binoculars in the direction of Tyldesley.

"It's here now!" He shouted, "I can see it!"

Harry's heart began to pound as he heard the sound of a whistle as the train passed through 'Jackson's Sidings' half a mile down the track.

The boy with the binoculars shouted again. "It's not the '*Flying Scotsman*'," amidst some cries of disappointment, but it did not bother Harry. He was going to savour the moment.

Distant sounds of 'ssh, ssh ssh' could be heard as the great locomotive thundered towards them, smoke billowing from its stack and white steam hissing around its wheels. Those close to the track, stepped back a few paces as the train drew near. Suddenly, it was upon them. Harry looked up in wonderment and saw the gleaming locomotive in its green and black colours; the highly polished brass nameplate displayed the words 'THE ROYAL SCOT'.

A great emotion came over him; his eyes moistened. He felt humble at first, and then proud - proud to have witnessed such a sight as this. It was even a greater moment than when he had displayed his mother's fine china pottery at the school party. He marvelled at how anyone could make such a machine as this; so powerful that it could haul many carriages at great speed. He wished he could become an engine driver when he grew up, or perhaps an engineer, able to make one of these wonderful machines.

Someone from the driver's cab waved to the crowd as the train passed by, no one knew whether it was the driver or fireman, as there were reports of there being four people in the cab. Twelve carriages hauled by the great locomotive were filled with people, some of them waving to the crowd as the train disappeared into the distance. The moment was over, but Harry's friends congregated together to discuss what they had seen and to await the arrival of the 4.20 PM, which was usually another named locomotive.

Harry sped off home, he was already late for Mrs Timperley's errands, but even this went well for him that day. He managed to get the full quota of cigarettes for the Timperley brothers, this meant his spending money was assured for the next few weeks.

He went to bed that evening and thought of the wonderful day he had had ... These were happy days indeed.

CHANGING TIMES

In the late spring months of 1950, Harry Hudson and several other pupils in his class were told to make their choice about which senior school they wished to attend when they left junior school in a few weeks. It was a bit of a shock to Harry. For some strange reason, he had never given it much thought and he fully expected to be spending his next school year in standard four, taught by Miss Barrows' elder sister Elsie. Harry had looked forward to going into standard four, as he had a feeling that Elsie Barrow was less strict than her sister Ethel and maybe he would learn some basketwork which she taught to a few select pupils. However he had become less enthusiastic when he learned Elsie Barrows' pet subject was Mathematics. He was also puzzled by the fact that some of his classmates would not be leaving junior school but would go up into standard four for their next year. It was explained to him that he was only eligible to go to senior school by the narrowest of margins.

In North West Britain, the annual summer holidays began in the last week of June and the new school term started in the first week of August. This period was known as 'Wakes Week' therefore, any days between the first to the seventh of August could be the start of the new term. That particular year, the new school term started on the 4th of August, which was Harry's birthday. It was decided that, as he was eleven years old on the day, he could therefore attend senior school; but two of his friends, whose birthdays were on the sixth and seventh of that month, were told to stay on for another year at junior school.

The system was changed shortly after this, allowing pupils to leave junior school in December and start senior school in January. Harry was now looking forward to attending senior school. He had already made his choice; his new school was to be The Hermitage-Fulwood Secondary Modern School.

The last few days in Miss Ethel Barrows' standard three class were fairly easy for those few pupils who were leaving. They were told to write an essay all about themselves and not to bother too much about other lessons. At the same time, almost all of Miss Elsie Barrows' standard four class were doing the same, except for a small group who had passed their 'eleven plus' and were going on to Grammar school. The purpose of the essay was to assess each pupil's standard of education, so they could be appropriately placed in different grades at senior school.

Harry wrote about his home and family; he also went on to describe his errand job and his time spent in Uncle Jack's house. He gave a brief description of his interests as: train-spotting, history, looking at old objects and the occasional football or cricket match. He had mentioned football and cricket just to keep in step with what he knew most of the other boys in his class would include as *their* interests; in reality, he was not very good at these sports.

As the weeks dragged on to the summer break, Harry began to feel a proper sense of change as events began to unfold around him. He had been told to take his younger brother John with him whenever he did Mrs Timperley's errands. It soon became obvious to him that John was being groomed to take over his job, as he realised the bus journey from his new school would take time. It would be well past 4 PM when he would arrive home. In view of this, Mrs Timperley had decided to hand over the job to John. Harry had mixed feelings about this; on the one hand, he would not be on call between the hours of 4 PM and 6 PM and would be free to go with his friends – train-spotting or whatever, on the other hand, he would have no spending money and would have to do without life's little luxuries.

One morning after school prayers in the assembly hall, Mr Bardsley began to walk up to the platform, as the last notes of '*He Who Would Valiant Be*' were being painfully extracted from an ancient piano by Elsie Barrow. After the final notes had died down, Mr Bardsley smiled at her and nodded his approval of her rendering of the famous hymn. He stood on the platform, cleared his throat and bid silence. He spoke in loud clear tones.

"It is with regret that I have to tell you I am retiring after many years of teaching at this school. They were happy years indeed and I shall miss you all."

He went on to describe a number of incidents and recited a few amusing tales of his experiences over the years. He finally ended: "Nothing lasts forever, times change and we have to accept and embrace change, put our best foot forward and make the best of it."

Harry was tinged with sadness at first but then he began to feel a degree of comfort from Mr Bardsley's words. After all, there was no point in dwelling on the fact that he would not see Mr Bardsley again; this would be the case even if Mr Bardsley was not retiring.

Harry began to make the most of his free time as his younger brother John took over Mrs Timperley's errands about two weeks before the annual summer holidays began.

One afternoon at 4 PM, after school, Harry and his friends decided to go to the L.Y.R.C. railway line at a place called Shackleton Lane Bridge, it turned out to be an incident that would land him and his friends in serious trouble.

A number of 'namers' were known to pass through this area between the hours of 4 and 6 PM. They had arrived at the track at 4.15 PM and in the space of about 30 minutes they had managed to see two fairly rare 'namers' and three other numbered locos to add to their collection. There were two or three other groups of schoolboys a short distance away and some of these were venturing quite close to the track.

Suddenly there were loud shouts of: "Clear off, clear off, or I will get the police onto you."

Harry and his friends turned to the direction of the shouting to find it had come from the signal-man, who by this time had made his way onto the observation platform of the signal box in an effort to make himself seen and heard. Most of the other boys disappeared quickly, but Harry and his friends remained where they were, egged on by one of the older boys telling them that the signal-man dare not leave his box and was of no threat to them.

As time went by, other groups of train-spotters took up their positions alongside the track and the signal-man's pleas were ignored as two more trains sped past amid cheers of enthusiasm from everyone. Shortly after this, a stranger appeared on the scene and made his way towards Harry and his friends, ignoring anyone else who happened to be close by. They thought it was strange because the man was well into his fifties and he was riding a cycle of the type which was normally used by grocers' boys for deliveries. Relieved that he was not a policeman, the boys soon took him into their confidence as he began to ask them questions.

"Are you getting 'namers' boys?"

"Yes," was the reply.

"Aye it's a grand hobby, I used to do it myself when I was your age. Did you get the twenty past fourer and the half-past fourer?"

"Yes," they chorused.

"What were they?" said the stranger.

"POLYPHEMUS and the GREEN HOWARDS" they all blurted out proudly.

"Well I never! They are rare them two. I don't think I ever managed to get them; a 'Jub' and a 'Scot' if I remember correctly."

The boys were pleased that an adult was taking such an interest in their hobby. Besides that, he seemed to know quite a lot about train-spotting; perhaps they could learn something from him.

They began to ask him questions such as: 'What was the rarest 'namer' he ever saw?' and 'what class was such a locomotive?' etc. He always gave them an answer which proved correct when they looked in their books. Harry eyed the man up and down. There was something familiar with the clothes he wore; he knew he had seen this type of man somewhere else.

He looks very much like Dick Barton thought Harry; he has the same type of 'Trilby' hat and long, gabardine mackintosh.

Dick Barton was a popular private detective featured in a radio broadcast almost every evening; he also appeared in comic books in the late 1940's. There was nothing special about brown trilbies and long, gabardine macs., but for some strange reason it seemed to be the standard dress for all detectives at that time.

Harry became more suspicious when the man kept looking at his watch and writing a few notes in a small book he had produced from the inside pocket of his coat. Another man suddenly appeared on the scene. He was dressed in a railway uniform with a badge bearing the letters L.Y.R.C. on his cap. The badge was obviously out of date, because the rest of his uniform bore the new crest of British Railways. He exchanged a few words with the other man and the two of them began to talk in hushed tones as they compared notes, written in small books, with each other.

Harry sensed there was something wrong and began to wish he was elsewhere. The man with the 'Trilby' turned to face the boys and said: "Right. I'll have all your names and addresses if you don't mind. Trespassing on the railway is a serious offence you know." He went on "I suppose you know you are all in trouble?"

The boys were shocked into silence for a few moments... and then one of them spoke up. "Please sir, could you let us off and we will not do it again?"

"Ha, ha," he muttered, "now where have I heard all that before?"

The man with the railway uniform instructed the boys to follow him, whilst the other man, whom the boys had realised by now, was a plain clothes policeman or detective, followed on at the rear. The boys were marched about half a mile into the town of Atherton and were relieved when they saw they were being taken to the local railway station, not the police station.

They were met at the station by another uniformed railway employee who gleefully shouted, "I see you've rounded the buggers up!"

The boys were led into a small room which had an ancient candlestick telephone hung on the wall, surrounded by timetables and posters of holiday resorts, 'Happy Days Ahead', 'Enjoy Your Holidays And Go By British Railways' etc. The door was shut behind them and the boys were left on their own for a few minutes to discuss their fate.

The door re-opened and in walked the detective with a bespectacled little man who began to recite all the times of the passing trains for the last two hours. The telephone rang; it was answered by the little man, who was probably a railway clerk.

"It's for you. It's from the signal-man at Shackleton Lane Bridge" said the clerk, as he handed the phone to the detective.

A brief conversation followed, ended by the detective saying: "I've got five of the buggers here now. I think I've got the right ones." He then addressed the boys."Now then, we will go over your details again and don't tell me no lies, or you will be in more serious trouble than you are now."

He tested the boys' statements of their names and addresses, their ages and the name of their school by asking them about various landmarks, the names of their teachers and other details. He was reasonably satisfied they had answered him truthfully; he also had evidence of how long they had been at the railway track, from the information they had given him of the passing trains that afternoon.

"I am going to let you go home, I expect your parents will be wondering where you all are, it's well past six," he said. "But you have not heard the last of this. We shall be taking the matter further and your parents will hear from us shortly."

With that, he opened the door of the clerk's office and told them to go straight home. As they made their way out of the station, they could hear an engine hissing steam. It was the 6.55 train that had stopped to allow passengers off after their day's work in the city.

One of the boys piped up "I wonder if that is a 'namer'?"

"We are not even bothered," came the overwhelming reply from the rest of them.

On their way home, they discussed how they would make the situation known to their parents. Harry felt physically sick in the pit of his stomach. He was scared of what his father would say. His father had often warned him about getting into trouble and said if a policeman ever came to the house because of him, then his life would not be worth living.

"Why didn't we run when the detective first came?" asked one of the boys.

"Because we didn't know he was a detective" came the reply from someone else.

"We should have done," said Harry, "He had a brown trilby on and all detectives have brown trilbies. "

"No they don't. My granddad's got a brown trilby, and he used to be a tram driver."

"Oh shut up will you! How was any of us to know? He fooled us all by coming on a grocer's bike and that's what detectives do – they trick you. They are clever, that's why they are detectives." These words came from the oldest boy - who was thirteen – and put an end to the argument.

When Harry reached home, his mother Kitty wanted to know where he had been. "You were never this late when you did Mrs Timperley's errands" she said.

Harry wished he was *still* doing Mrs Timperley's errands; he would not be in this situation now. "I've been to Shackleton Lane Bridge, train-spotting. I didn't know it was this time." he said.

"Your tea is going cold. Better get it eaten now while I cook your father's meal," said Kitty.

Harry was relieved his father was not home. He often worked a couple of hours overtime. This would be a chance for him to confide his situation with his mother. He had no proper appetite to eat his evening meal, so he decided there and then to tell her of his situation.

"I am late because I have been in trouble," he blurted out, his voice trembling.

"What kind of trouble?" Kitty asked with alarm.

"We have been caught trespassing on the railway at Shackleton Lane Bridge," said Harry.

He told her of the other four boys he was with. Kitty knew all of them and was on quite friendly terms with most of their mothers.

"I've told you before that Kenneth Halton is too old for you, he is nearly fourteen!" she shrieked. "Did you go onto the track?"

"No, but Kenneth Halton did," said Harry.

"Did you climb through the fence?"

"Yes," replied Harry.

"Then you are all in the same boat and I think we will be hearing from the police about this!" she shouted.

This was confirmed by Harry when he told her the detective had said 'You have not heard the last of this'. Their conversation was interrupted by the sound of clogs on stone flags.

"Go into the front room and read your comics, your father's here now," said Kitty.

Harry left the kitchen whilst his mother began to serve up his father's evening meal. He tried to listen in on the conversation between them, but it appeared to be just small talk, with no mention of the day's events. Harry went to bed that evening and did not sleep very well. His thoughts were of how things could change so quickly and completely alter your whole way of life. Just a few days ago, he did not know he would be changing schools, lose his errand job, or might never see Mr Bardsley again. All these things had now come to reality. On top of this, he was in serious trouble with the police.

Things went fairly well at school next day, there was a relaxed atmosphere. End of term examinations were completed and Harry's class were told to do some reading of their own choice. Harry chose a book from the classroom library, which was a couple of old desks nailed together and stocked with old canvas-backed books, some of them dating back to Victorian times.

Ethel Barrow had created the library and stocked it with storybooks carefully chosen to interest most children. It was a way of escape from normal school lessons. It worked quite well for both pupils and teacher. Miss Barrow would put it to use when she was too busy or could not be bothered to teach a lesson. Surprisingly, the librarian was a boy who had often been in trouble; his new-found position gave him a sense of responsibility and importance and he became a model pupil. Harry went up to the library and asked the boy in charge if he could borrow 'The Magic Ragman'. The boy rummaged through a pile of books and produced a canvas-backed small book which had seen better days.

"What do you want this for? It's only for seven year olds."

"Jimmy Collins said I would like this book," said Harry.

"Jimmy Collins," sneered the other boy. "He can't even read properly."

The statement was quite true. Jimmy Collins could barely read. He had spent more days at home than he had at school. His parents had been in trouble on more than one occasion over his truancy, but in the last few weeks they had enforced his attendance in a desperate bid to prepare him for senior school, Apparently it had taken Jimmy two weeks to read the book, which contained only forty pages of *very* large print with a few illustrations. Even this had been under the supervision of Miss Barrow who had spent a few minutes with him each lesson, teaching him to spell words that contained no more than seven letters.

Harry took the book back to his desk and read through it quite quickly. It was all about a rag man who trundled an old hand-cart through the streets. He blew through a battered old trumpet to attract people's attention. But this was no ordinary trumpet; the notes that came from it were formed into magical tunes, the like of which people had never heard before. The music cast a spell over the people and influenced them to part with their most valued possessions in exchange for a few pots, a goldfish in a bowl or a couple of rubbing stones.

Rubbing stones were used by Northern people to put a white finish on their door steps and were normally given by the rag man in exchange for a bundle of old rags. Harry was more interested in the illustrations in the book, rather than the story. The rag man's cart was piled high with wonderful objects which he had fooled people into parting with. A chest of drawers looked very much like the one he and his friends had thrown onto the bonfire; an old grandfather clock and a 'Vienna Regulator' and various other clocks, together with an assortment of beautifully coloured fine china, pottery and bric-a-brac were wonderfully illustrated in the book.

Harry had temporarily forgotten his problems whilst reading the book, but the sound of the bell to end school lessons for that day soon jolted him back into reality. He went home that afternoon with time on his hands and trouble on his mind. He could no longer do Mrs Timperley's errands; at least this would have killed some of the time. He could go to Uncle Jack's house, but he thought his melancholy mood would arouse suspicion and Uncle Jack would ask him awkward questions regarding his peculiar behaviour.

He decided to read 'The Dandy' – this was his favourite comic, together with its sister comic 'The Beano', they were the most popular comics of the day. He forgot himself for a while, enjoying the escapades of 'Desperate Dan', 'Hungry Horace', 'Old Ma Murphy', and other characters. His mind drifted away until he turned the pages to read the story of 'Black Bob'.

'Black Bob' was a sheepdog who lived with his master, Andrew Glenn in the Scottish Highlands. He was an extremely clever animal who, with his master, always managed to get caught up in some kind of adventure whilst tending the sheep. The illustration to the story that particular week, was of the famous sheepdog and his master apprehending a villain, whilst a burly policeman struggled to get handcuffs on him. The very sight of the policeman caused Harry to feel sick in the pit of his stomach. He now realised if the police wanted you, you were usually in some kind of trouble.

A sharp knock on the front door made him almost jump out of his skin. His nerves jangled and he hesitated as he tried to compose himself. He looked around him to see if anyone else in the house would answer the door, but everyone seemed to be out. Again he heard another two or three sharp raps on the door, this time even louder. He decided to answer it, in the hope it would be one of his friends, but his worse fears came true as he stared into the eyes of a policeman.

"Is your father or mother in?"

"I'll see if I can find my mother," stuttered Harry, his voice trembling with fear.

He dashed through the kitchen and into the communal backyard to find his mother collecting washing from the clothes line and chatting to two other women who were doing the same. He told her there was someone at the front door to see her and she immediately followed him. Kitty was rather shocked to see a policeman, even though she had half-expected it. She quickly invited him into the house and then looked out into the street, hoping the neighbours hadn't seen who the visitor was.

She shut and locked the door behind her. The policeman removed his helmet, which made Harry feel a lot less nervous. A brief conversation followed, between Kitty and the officer and he presented her with a document which they both signed.

As he turned to leave the house, he looked at Harry and said: "I hope you are keeping out of trouble young man."

"Yes sir," came the reply.

When the policeman had gone, Kitty told Harry that things were moving very fast. The police were going to prosecute on behalf of the railway.

"I have not even told your father yet, and they have already set a date for you all to appear at Juvenile Court," she said.

Harry was now beginning to wish his father *did* know, because sooner or later, he would have to.

"I will tell your father tonight, try to calm him down and hope this will be the end of the matter," said Kitty.

Harry felt a little better after hearing this and was even prepared to accept a few strokes of his fathers leather razor strap across his backside if it would get the matter over and done with.

The closing days at school were fairly uneventful, except it had become known that Harry and his friends had to appear in court for trespassing on the railway. A couple of them had openly boasted about the incident and this had lost no time in circulating throughout the school. Miss Barrow rebuked any tittle-tattle coming from other pupils who had hoped their stories would get the boys into further trouble.

"I do not want to hear about those boys who are in trouble!" she shouted, "Other people will deal with them shortly."

Harry wondered whether the 'other people' would include his new teachers at senior school, as well as the local magistrates. At last, junior school was over and Harry went home that afternoon and wondered what the future had in store for him.

That very same evening, his father confronted him with a really severe lecture about getting into trouble.

"What did I tell you about getting into trouble with the police?"

His tones grew angrier and louder as Harry listened with respect, fearful of what the final punishment would be. His father ended by saying he had not to go much further than the end of the street for the next few weeks.

His ordeal was over. He had fully expected to get at least half-a-dozen strokes of the razor strap, a punishment he had had in the past for much lesser offences. The long summer break drifted on and Harry did as he was told.

He had temporarily lost his appetite for collecting 'namers' and spent most of the time on Uncle Jack's allotment. His mother had made close contact with the other boys' mothers to discuss the arrangements of their sons appearance in court, which had been set for the end of July.

The timing was very convenient; just one week before, all the boys (except Kenneth Halton) were due to start at the same senior school – Hermitage Fulwood Secondary Modern. The biggest problem the mothers had on their minds was the possibility of a hefty fine. Money was scarce; there were several children in each family and only one worker. However, all of them had come into a little income of their own quite recently. The government had introduced family allowance for each child in the family, except the eldest. The allowance was five shillings per child. Harry's mother claimed for his two sisters and two brothers, which amounted to one pound (twenty shillings). She had managed to save a few shillings each week to help to pay for Harry's fine.

One evening, as the day of their appearance in court drew nearer, she asked Harry's father how much he thought the fine would be. For some strange reason he was laughing. and appeared to be quite amused.

"You have changed your tune these last few days," she snapped. "It was a serious business a few days ago."

Still laughing, he pointed at Harry. "He should know. Anyone who trespasses on the railway should have seen the black and white cast iron signs that says 'you will be fined forty shillings'. More so, the signs were put up in Victorian times, so I expect it will be more than that in these times."

"Oh dear, I hope it is not," said Kitty, "It's no laughing matter you know."

But Dick Hudson was laughing at something else now. "I should imagine it is going to he very embarrassing if they ask you which school you go to?" he chortled.

"Why?" said Kitty.

"Because one of the magistrates will be Mrs Fulwood who is a member of the family who founded the school," said Dick, who could barely contain himself by now.

Harry had a feeling that everything was going to be alright, especially as his father was making fun of the situation.

The day of the court hearing finally arrived, and their appearance was timed for 11.30 AM. All the boys and their mothers arrived at court and were told to wait in a room until they were called. They were eventually called into a wooden panelled room, the mothers were told to sit down and the boys were told to stand up and face a large bench which had three seats occupied by two men and one woman.

The man in the centre spoke first. He went on to underline the foolishness of trespassing on the railway and the consequences that it could lead to. The lady magistrate endorsed his statement and gave a brief speech urging the boys to keep out of trouble in the future. The other magistrate said nothing but began to write notes in a book. There were no members of the public in court, except two officials who were also making notes.

The man in the centre rose to his feet and addressed Kenneth Halton, the eldest boy. "From what I have gathered, you are the ringleader and at nearly fourteen years of age you should have set a better example." He went on: "When the signalman told you to clear off, you encouraged the others to stay by telling them that they were safe because the signalman dare not leave his signal box therefore he could not catch you. You silly boy! Have you never heard of a telephone?"

The magistrate sat back in his seat and then there was a prolonged conversation between the three of them. This was an anxious period of time for the boys and their mothers as they all wondered what the punishment would be. Finally, the chairman of the magistrates rose to his feet and addressed them.

"It is the finding of this court, that all five boys are guilty of trespassing on the railway and are found to be in breach of railway by-laws under section six of the L.Y.R.C. rules. You will *all* have to pay a fine of five shillings each."

He then paused for a while before continuing, "But you must remember if any one of you come before this court again, then you will be more severely dealt with."

He then thanked the boys' mothers for their co-operation, saying he was satisfied that all the boys had come from good homes and he believed they had all learned their lesson. He then dismissed them all, and a court official invited the mothers to his desk to settle the fines.

Once outside, all the party had feelings of relief and they began to discuss how leniently they had been dealt with. Kitty was extremely pleased with her new found wealth. She had saved the sum of two pounds ten shillings towards the fine. All of them were in high spirits, it was as though a black cloud had passed over them. To make things even better, one of the mothers suggested they all go to a café and have lunch; after all, they could all afford it with the extra money they now had. This was greeted wholeheartedly as all the women burst into laughter.

It was the first time Harry had ever been into a café. A bright feeling came over him as he tucked into beef sandwiches and buttered scones. At home that evening, Harry had another stern lecture from his father, after he had heard of the court's warning regarding any future trouble. The whole matter was now over and done with, he had indeed learned his lesson and was now back on a level footing. He went to bed that evening in high spirits and began to look forward to what the future had in store for him.

SENIOR SCHOOL

It was late July and there was still a few days to go before Harry would start the new school term at Hermitage Fulwood Secondary Modern. He was spending his time doing the things he was used to; taking long walks in the countryside, chatting to his friends, playing games and swapping comics. When he was not doing this, he would be in Uncle Jack's house questioning him about the 'olden days'. It was on one such occasion that he answered a loud knock on the door.

"See who it is," said Uncle Jack, who could not be bothered to look up from the racing section of the 'Daily Herald'.

Harry answered the door and was greeted by a smartly dressed little man holding a suitcase.

"Good afternoon. Is there someone older in the house I could speak to about clocks and watches?"

Harry shouted back to Uncle Jack, "It's a man who wants to know about clocks and watches."

"Come inside!" shouted Uncle Jack.

The stranger stepped inside and Harry closed the door behind him. The man was told to sit down and declare his interest.

"I believe you have a very good 'Vienna Regulator' and a silver chronograph pocket watch," said the man.

"Who told you that?" asked Uncle Jack, who was not too pleased for a stranger to know such things.

"A man living around the corner in Lord Street," came the reply.

"Aye. Bill Underwood will have told you. It would not do for him to know too much." Uncle Jack responded.

Bill Underwood and Uncle Jack were the best of friends, but they often criticised each other over their differences. This was a time when a man's pocket watch was a status symbol among working-class men. Uncle Jack held pride in the knowledge that he was reputed to have the finest pocket watch in the village; if he could be relieved of it, then perhaps Bill Underwood would then hold this accolade.

"Can I see them?" asked the stranger.

Uncle Jack removed his watch from his waistcoat pocket and placed it on the table. It was his pride and joy. "I paid seven sovereigns for it in 19 18 and it was second hand then!" he proudly exclaimed.

The stranger, who by this time had declared himself to be a dealer in antiques and jewellery, carefully picked up the watch and flicked open the back cover. He studied a few markings on the inside of the lid and then inserted a pen-knife into the second cover and opened it.

"Ah ah," he muttered. "You don't see so many of these. It was made by Henry Bernstein of Manchester; it is 64 years old and the eighteen jewel movement shows no signs of wear whatsoever. Would you be interested in selling it?"

"I don't think so, I have had it all these years and don't want to part with it at my time of life."

"I will give you a very good price for it," said the dealer.

"What do you call a good price?" Uncle Jack retorted.

Harry was now sitting in a chair at the other end of the room whilst the two men did their business. He strained his ears in the hope he would hear a large sum of money offered for the watch. To his disappointment, the dealer scribbled his offer for the watch onto a piece of notepaper and handed it to Uncle Jack.

The old man looked stunned. He took off his glasses and wiped them, then put them back on and had another look at the paper.

"As much as that?" said Uncle Jack.

"Yes, as much as that," replied the dealer.

There was quite a long period of silence between the two of them...

Uncle Jack spoke first. "It is a very good offer, but I have had it all these years and I do not really want to part with it."

"Very well, if that is your wish, then so be it. Now what about the 'Vienna Regulator'?" said the dealer.

"No, I don't think so. It belonged to my mother," said Uncle Jack, whose real excuse was not wanting strangers walking through his bedroom, where the clock had hung for many years. Not wanting to entirely dampen the dealer's interest, he offered to show him some of the books in the display cabinet.

Uncle Jack opened the cabinet and placed a few books onto the table. The dealer quickly looked at the books and placed a few to one side.

46

"What about 'Pilgrims Progress' which is still in the cabinet?" he said.

"You cannot have that even if you offer me a hundred pounds" said Uncle Jack.

Harry was stunned. It was too much of a sum of money to contemplate; the greatest sum of money he had ever possessed was two shillings and eight pence.

"Oh come now," said the dealer "I could make you a very good offer. It would not be quite as much as that, but I think we could come to some agreement."

"Not for sale," said Uncle Jack as he now realised the book was *very* valuable.

"Then what about the carved snake and crocodile and the two lizards on the sideboard?"

"The lizards are ivory you know," said Uncle Jack.

"Yes. Yes, I know. I will give you quite a few pounds for them if you are interested," replied the dealer.

"No, they are not for sale. They were left to me by a very dear friend," said Uncle Jack.

"Very well then. How much will you take for the books?"

Uncle Jack was at a loss regarding the value of the books, but he was prepared to sell them and asked the dealer to make him an offer. The dealer selected a few of the books and wrote his offer for each of them on a sheet of notepaper.

Uncle Jack looked at the paper and said: "Take them."

With that, the dealer opened his suitcase and placed the books inside. He reached into his pockets and handed Uncle Jack a few pound notes and some silver coins. He then bid good day and went on to his next port of call.

"Well, that's that. We can use a bit of extra money and the books were doing nowt anyway," said Uncle Jack as he resumed his study of the horseracing section of his newspaper.

Harry went home and began to think how a few old books could be worth so much money, but it was no good looking around his own home, there were none.

He soon forgot about the sale of the books, although he had mentioned it to his parents, especially the £100 figure Uncle Jack was prepared to refuse for 'Pilgrims Progress'. His thoughts were now focussed on what life would be like at senior school in a few days time.

Some of his older friends had told him that he would probably go straight into A1, the highest form for first year. Harry did not set his sights so high, mainly to avoid disappointment. He would be quite content to be placed in B1. The worst case scenario would be: being placed in C group - this was a class that embraced *all* age groups of the least educated pupils. Some of them were difficult cases whose needs would be dealt with by special schools in later years, but these were the austere years of the early fifties, and you had to make the best of it.

The big day finally arrived. It was the first Wednesday in August; for some strange reason the new term after the long summer break always started on a Wednesday. Was it because the teachers could not face a full week in the job after enjoying their six-week summer break?.

Harry and his friends arrived at the new school after a one mile bus journey costing a halfpence each way. The fare was increased to a three halfpence return shortly after, effectively putting a farthing extra charge on each journey. Farthings were no longer in use, but this was the bus company's only means of imposing a fare increase, the first for fifty years, amidst complaints from the public who saw it as a 50% increase, such was travel in those days.

After morning assembly in the school hall, established pupils were told to make their way to their new classrooms, the new intake of pupils were told to stay where they were to await their name being called. After what seemed an eternity, Harry's name was finally called and he was told to go to room 1A; he was pointed in the right direction to his new classroom by a school monitor.

Once inside the classroom, he was told to be seated at any vacant desk and this would be his permanent position for all lessons in that classroom. The few remaining desks were soon occupied by a steady trickle of boys coming in, the door was closed, and the teacher bid them all "Good Morning."

"Good Morning Sir," came the reply - loud and clear, at which the teacher smiled his approval.

"I see you are all wide-eyed and awake, I hope you keep like that. My name is Mr Harper, but you shall address me as 'Sir'."

He went on to tell them he was their form master and his teaching subjects were, Geometry, Religious Instruction, English, Maths and Sports. Harry was still in a state of bewilderment, he could hardly believe he had been able to get into an 'A Form". His

48

eyes wandered around the room and he soon recognised a few of his old friends from junior school. He knew most of them had come from Elsie Barrow's standard four class at junior school and they would he more knowledgeable about maths and geometry than he was. Harry began to think it was no big deal getting into an 'A Form', and maybe anyone of average intelligence could do it.

But what about Jimmy Collins?. Harry suddenly realised he was not in the classroom. Well, he may have made it into a 'B Form'.

"Right. Now," said Mr Harper, "Open your desks and get out your drawing board, 'T' square, set squares and compasses and we will start our first lesson in Geometry."

The Geometry lesson occupied the rest of the morning until midday break and the whole afternoon was taken up with an Art lesson in another room, given by a Scotsman called Mr Buchan.

On their way home after school, Harry and his friends discussed how easy their first day had been. Most of them had managed to make it into 1A, some only made it to 1B and Jimmy Collins and a couple of other boys joined the dreaded C Group. Everyone had been given a timetable of lessons to take home and study at their leisure, it helped them to mentally prepare for the lessons in advance.

As the days passed, Harry looked forward to two lessons in particular – Woodwork and Science. The first lesson in Science proved a little disappointing. He had expected to learn all about space travel and landing on the Moon. These were the subjects he had read about in his comics, where space ships were launched by scientists who had built them in their own laboratories; but the lesson was all about magnetism and electricity. the class were given a practical demonstration, where two magnets were placed close to each other and their positions reversed to demonstrate their attraction and repellent forces. Some boys seemed quite enthralled by the experiment, but Harry was rather bored. He had done this little experiment for himself with two magnets he had taken from an old radio which he had rescued from last year's bonfire.

The Woodwork lesson proved to be more interesting, especially when the teacher held up various tools and asked if anyone could name them. He had seen some of the same type in Uncle Jack's shed and held up his hand in the hope that he would be given the opportunity to answer. Several other boys did the same.

"Alright, alright, I can see a few of you are familiar with woodworking tools, let's hope there is a Chippendale or Hepplewhite among you," he said.

He then went on to give a brief talk about the two great eighteenth century furniture makers and ended by saying today's furniture was more or less 'plywood rubbish'.

Harry Corlish had been woodwork master at the school since the early thirties. He was a 'dapper' little man who wore a waistcoat and armbands and was quite a bit older than the other teachers. Harry took an immediate liking to him; both of them had the same Christian names and his black serge waistcoat and armbands reminded him of his own father, who wore exactly the same. Harry was even more pleased when Mr Corlish told them that better furniture was being thrown onto bonfires than could be bought at the present time.

As the weeks passed by, Harry settled into senior school but was troubled by a few subjects he knew he was not doing very well, especially mathematics. He noticed nearly all the boys who had been in standard four class at junior school were doing better than him. However, he soon realised that history lessons were his best chance of gaining high marks, which would prevent him from finishing near the bottom of the class at exams. He had been commended several times by Mr Morton for giving the correct answers to a number of questions on the 'Middle Ages'. More so, on a number of occasions, he had been the only person in the whole class to attempt to answer a question and this had made him Mr Morton's 'favourite'. He could just get by on English and Geography and had begun to come to terms with and eventually like, French lessons. However Sports and Physical Training caused him problems and he was well down the list with these two subjects; the main reasons for this were lack of confidence and lack of stature. Most of the other boys were much taller and heavier than him and it was soon noticed that the boys from his Junior School had never been taught sports.

Harry and some of his friends from Junior School were fast becoming the butt of jokes when it became known they had been taught knitting, yes.. knitting! What else could you expect coming from a school run by an all-female staff and one ageing headmaster too old to play sports?

As the weeks turned into months, Harry began to wish he was back at Junior School, where life had been much easier. His own teacher, Mr Harper, had told them that two or three boys were in danger of being relegated to a B Form if they did not improve on some subjects. The Mid-Term exams came and went and over the Christmas holidays Harry worried about possible relegation into 1B. Once again he was pleasantly surprised when he found himself in the same classroom when school re-started. However, he soon learned he had narrowly escaped relegation only by scoring a very high mark at History and this had boosted his low marks on most of the other subjects.

Mr Morton had placed him in second position in exams for History; first position had been given to a boy called David Potter. It was rumoured that David Potter was being groomed to attend a higher school because he was 'much cleverer' than the rest of the class. There was some degree of truth in this. He always seemed to get special attention from the other teachers. Harry's friends had dared to suggest that David Potter could not possibly have beaten him at History and his position may have been 'fixed' to satisfy his parents who were never away from the school, 'hob-knobbing' with the teachers. Harry was not really bothered, he was quite happy with the situation and enjoyed the prestige of coming second to David Potter. He was now satisfied that he was reasonably safe from relegation for some months and he would he able to catch up on some of the other subjects. In the meantime, he decided not to worry too much about school and concentrate on his old hobbies.

HARD TIMES

Harry's main problem now was lack of pocket money. His parents could not afford to give him any and he had no older brothers and sisters who were working and could afford to treat him. He was envious of his friends who often had pocket money given to them by an older brother or sister who wished to be rid of them whilst they carried on their courting.

He was especially envious of Jimmy Collins, who seemed to have everything (with the exception of proper teeth and an inability to read).Jimmy's teeth were completely rotten, due to having an inexhaustible supply of sweets. This seemed rather unusual, as sweets had been strictly rationed throughout the war years up until about 1951.Jimmy's inexhaustible supply of sweets could easily be explained by anyone who lived close by. There always seemed to be a constant stream of visitors to the house, laden with plain parcels or cardboard boxes. Either way, coming or going, everyone seemed to have a packet or parcel.

This practice had been going on since rationing had begun at the beginning of the war. Since Jimmy's dad seemed to have no proper job, it was reasoned by many that he must be running a 'Black Market'. Also Jimmy's sister had a bit of a reputation for having too many boy friends. It was noticed that his sister's male friends were not local lads; they all came from around the Port of Liverpool, a distance of about twenty miles away. Even Jimmy's Granddad seemed to be in on the act. For many years he had supplied Harry's mother with soap powder and other household goods in exchange for toffee coupons. This explained the reasons why Harry and his brothers and sisters had very few sweets and why Jimmy Collins's teeth were falling out.

Not a week went by without Jimmy having something new, like an airgun, a wrist watch, or even a bicycle. Harry's ultimate dream was to own a bicycle – even a second hand one would do. Jimmy had had at least *five* new bicycles before he reached the age of twelve. Every time he came up the street on a new bike, Harry would be filled with envy and wonder how some people could be so lucky and others not. He would often complain to his parents about the unfairness of it all; his mother would sympathise and be apologetic to him for not having the means to help him. Harry's father's answer to the problem was always the same.

"We don't have to be bloody clever to know where the money is coming from in that household."

Harry decided he would have to find a way of earning some money, but money was very scarce in his part of the world ...and people did not part with it easily.

The ideal situation would be to get a job as a paper boy. Some of his older friends already had and the going rate for that job was ten shillings per week. He made a few enquiries at local newsagents shops, but was disappointed to learn you had to be thirteen years old to do the job. However, one shop keeper said she would put his name down for a paper delivery round which would become vacant in a few days time.

In the meantime he decided to sell firewood. He had done this before, with one of his friends and they had earned a few shillings. Harry mentioned his plan to one of his schoolmates, Fred Jones.

"I have already got a job on the pig farm. I get five bob for working an hour every night after school, but I can earn a bit extra if I go knocking on doors and asking them for their potato peelings, which we use to make pig swill from," said Fred.

Harry suggested that they could combine selling firewood and collecting potato peelings at the same time. The idea worked well; in fact most of the village had become trained to save their vegetable peelings for them. Harry and Fred met all kinds of people when they were knocking on doors to sell their firewood. Most of their customers were elderly retired people, who sometimes asked them in for a cup of tea and a chat. Sometimes they would be asked if they could supply coal as well as firewood, so the pair of them decided to supplement their income by supplying a few bags of coal to their best customers.

This was a slightly more difficult task. It meant a four mile round trip to one of the colliery spoil tips and the two of them spending several hours selecting good pieces of coal from the waste to fill two large sacks; which were then loaded onto Fred's old bike for a two mile journey to the customer. It was a very difficult and disheartening task for two young boys to manhandle sacks of coal which were heavier than themselves, especially when the customer disputed the weight of the coal inside the sacks. They would then be given four shillings for each sack of coal on the assumption they were underweight (the normal going rate for a sack of coal weighing a hundredweight (112 pounds) was five shillings). Nevertheless, Harry and Fred had to put up with being underpaid for their efforts. They had little choice in the matter if they wished to make some spending money.

They were quite happy with their little enterprise and got involved in some amusing situations which they would remember for the rest of their lives. On one occasion, they were invited into the home of an elderly man who had bought some firewood from them. Their Curiosity had been aroused by the sound of birds whistling and chattering.

"Do you keep budgies?" they asked.

"No. But I do keep birds. Come inside and you can see them," said the man.

Harry and Fred stepped inside the house and were amazed at what they saw. There were no carpets or linoleum on the floor, just flagstones. The only pieces of furniture in the room were an old rocking chair near the fireplace and a table; the rest of the room was taken up by bird cages stacked from floor to ceiling.

The cages were made from bicycle spokes and orange boxes and most of them were occupied by an assortment of birds such as house sparrows, thrushes, blackbirds, tits, etc.

"These are my feathered friends," said the old man. "Some of them are lame, but I try to nurse them back to health and release them." He then opened most of the cages and allowed the birds to fly about the house.

Harry and Fred were enthralled for the best part of an hour as the old man sat in the rocking chair and played a concertina whilst the birds sang and fluttered about an old tree which was supported through a hole in the centre of the table. The old man seemed to have a magical control over the birds; influenced by the tempo of the music he was playing. They responded most actively to sea shanties and fast jigs, but when he played a lullaby, the birds were calm and peaceful.

"Some of these birds don't really want to leave here, they have been with me for a long time," said the old man, as if justifying their capture.

There was probably some truth in this. The birds were warm, comfortable and well fed, but even so it was a unique situation, even for those days and certainly would not be allowed in present times, on the grounds of hygiene.

Harry's shortage of spending money was temporarily solved with the income from selling firewood and coal. Supplies of firewood were easy to come by. There were two old sheds on Uncle Jack's plot which had just been dismantled, so this would keep the firewood business going for a few weeks. Supplies of coal however, were a different matter.

Harry and Fred had begun to tire of the effort involved in transporting heavy bags of coal picked from colliery spoil tips in all weathers. It was common knowledge there was no shortage of coal in the village of Hindsford, in fact the whole village was built on a coalmine. A six foot high fence separated the colliery sidings from dozens of terraced houses occupied by the villagers. During the hours of daylight, hundreds of wagonloads of coal were filled at the mine and hauled over the railway sidings to a large building where the coal was washed and graded before being sold. This operation ceased when darkness fell, but wagons that had not reached their destination at the washing and grading plant remained stationary overnight in the railway sidings. This was a tempting situation for some of the villagers. It was no secret some of them made full use of the situation and were never short of coal, or money for that matter. Others were less fortunate and had been caught in the act; the usual punishment being a fine, and a 'ticking off' from the magistrates.

During the sale of some coal to one householder, Harry and Fred were asked where the coal had come from. When told they had legitimately hand picked it from the colliery spoil heap two miles away, he replied: "Good, but there are easier ways of doing it."

"Like what?" said Harry, who already knew where the other source of supply was.

"The colliery sidings of course! There is plenty of coal there and it is only a few yards from your home," replied the man.

"My dad says you should not steal coal from the colliery sidings because the owners are very kind to the villagers," said Harry.

"Ha ha. That's a good one coming from your dad! He has had more than his fair share of coal from there, but the crafty old bugger never got caught."

"But if we get caught, we could be expelled from school." Harry replied.

"Expelled from school? What do you mean?" he replied.

"We both go to Hermitage Fulwood Secondary Modern," said the pair of them.

"So what? That does not mean a thing today. Hermitage and Fulwood do not own the colliery any more, it was taken off them in 1948 and given to the National Coal Board. And rightly so! Damned upper class twits don't have a right to own everything and control our lives anymore!" said the householder.

Back home that evening, Harry told his father what he had learned that afternoon.

"Yes that's quite true. Hermitage and Fulwood do not own the colliery anymore, but you keep away from there my lad, because if you are caught stealing coal the new owners will not be as lenient with you as Hermitage and Fulwood would have been."

Hermitage and Fulwood were great benefactors to the village of Hindsford and the township of Atherton. They had built schools, houses and churches throughout the whole area and were the owners of several more collieries throughout the district. During strikes in the troubled times of the twenties and thirties, they fed and clothed the families of striking miners. They were also proud of the fact that working conditions in their mines were regarded as *'The best in the country'*, a statement coming from none other than the Prince of Wales, when he visited the collieries in the early thirties. So the villagers had a certain amount of respect for the former colliery owners, of which only two members of the Fulwood family now remained.

Old Major Fulwood lived in a rambling mansion on the outskirts of the village. The only other occupant in the house, apart from a couple of servants, was his sister-in-law, Mrs Mabel Fulwood - Magistrate and J.P.. They both saw themselves as 'Guardians Of The Peace' and were spending their remaining years visiting the schools they had built, ensuring the teachers were doing their jobs properly by upholding strict protestant beliefs and teaching the difference between right and wrong. But this was 1951 and most schools were state controlled and what was good for one, was the same for another.

Nevertheless, the Fulwood's still commanded a certain amount of respect and discipline throughout the district and pupils were known to have been expelled from their schools for minor offences. Harry had already met Mrs Fulwood, when he appeared before her in her capacity as a magistrate, after he was caught trespassing on the railway. He believed he had been given a chance to make good and he certainly did *not* wish to get into trouble again, so the very idea of stealing coal from the colliery railway sidings was out of the question.

Harry and Fred continued to run their little enterprise selling firewood and coal, but were disappointed to learn they were now faced with a little competition. Jimmy Collins's dad was seen with a horse and cart loaded with bags of firewood which he was delivering to a number of houses in the village. Harry and Fred were not pleased with this. How could they compete with sack loads of firewood when they only sold it by the bundle? They decided to follow the horse and cart from a safe distance, but were surprised and a little worried when they saw a couple of deliveries made to their own customers. Surely these customers would have asked them for more firewood if they were short? Stranger still, these same customers ordered their usual amount of firewood from them a few days later.

Jimmy's dad's firewood business seemed to have little effect on Harry and Fred's little enterprise, even several weeks later. Eventually, the horse and cart disappeared off the scene, along with their owner. No-one in the village had seen Jimmy's dad for several days.

It soon became known that Jimmy's dad and two more local men were in jail for stealing coal from the colliery sidings. They had been caught almost red-handed when police raided his Granddad's plot and looked inside two sheds. One of the sheds was full of firewood, but the other was full of coal. There was no harm in the firewood, anyone could sell firewood, but explaining where the coal had come from was a different matter, especially when it was less than twenty yards away from the colliery sidings. The firewood business was just a cover-up, literally. In fact, most of the sacks on the cart had been filled with coal and covered with a few sticks of firewood.

Jimmy's dad was not the first one to be caught stealing coal from the colliery sidings, but he was amongst the first to be caught stealing coal from the new owners, who were non other than the public themselves, now represented by 'The National Coal Board'. Had he been caught stealing coal from the previous owners, he would have been fined and given a stern lecture by the magistrates on the difference between right and wrong because the Fulwood's were reluctant to see any of the villagers going to jail.

In the aftermath of this, Jimmy Collins's lifestyle took a tumble downwards. He had previously enjoyed going to the cinema at least *six* times a week. Harry and the others had envied him as he told them stories of his great heroes 'Humphrey Bogart and James Cagney. Jimmy had sat in the cinema night after night, munching his favourite sweets – 'liquorice torpedoes'. He was now reduced to two visits per week to the cinema for the duration of his father's stay in one of H.M. prisons. Yes, even Jimmy had fallen upon hard times.

VILLAGE LIFE

Living in a pit village in Lancashire in the immediate post-war years could be a dull and drab experience, but you had to make the best of it. Very little had changed in Hindsford since before the war and most of the housing accommodation had remained unchanged since Victorian times. The population of 4,000 inhabitants lived in terraced houses and most of them had no hot water or electricity. If you had your own backyard you were reasonably fortunate, many of the houses had to share a communal backyard with other families and this could sometimes lead to arguments regarding each other's lifestyle.

For instance, there was usually a family that kept several pets and their owners allowed them to roam and do whatever they pleased, much to the annoyance of their neighbours. This usually led to a period of not speaking to each other, but because they were so close-knit, they were usually dependant on each other, especially in times of illness, so peace was eventually restored. The womenfolk did not usually fall out with each other because they shared a common bond. There was a limited number of clothes lines to be strung across a communal backyard and these had to be shared on washing day, which was always Monday. The ideal situation would have been to do the washing on different days, but different days were for other jobs and, since there were no washing machines that could be switched on at the touch of a button, Monday was washday.

It was a bit of a hectic situation if the coalman came on Monday. The housewives would be given a few seconds warning of impending peril to their handiwork by a loud shout of 'COAL', coming from a burly black-faced figure at the entrance to the backyard. Within seconds, doors were flung open and the housewives rushed out to retrieve their washing from the clothes line, each one helping the other to remove all the clothes as quickly as possible.

Tuesday was taken up airing and ironing the clothes, but this sometimes spread into Wednesday, especially in the winter months when the clothes had to be dried on a wooden clothes maiden around an open coal fire.

Thursday was the day for black-leading the fireplace grate with 'Zebo' polish and general cleaning throughout the house.

Friday was the day when housewives were expected to be on top of their chores and wearing a clean pinafore, ready to receive their husband's pay packet.

Saturday mornings were normally spent answering the door to callers who had come to collect payment for their services - the coalman, the milkman, newsagent, window cleaner, butcher's boy etc.; this was a time when, if you were owed money, you were advised to collect it before 12 noon, otherwise it would be spent elsewhere.

Saturday afternoon was the time when children went to the cinema matinee and their mothers took a well-earned break, having a bus ride into one of the larger towns to visit the department stores. The men folk usually worked on a Saturday morning and looked forward to a leisurely afternoon, perhaps going to a local football match, or listening to one on the radio, or betting on horseracing in a dingy house in a quiet corner of the village.

There was little respite for the housewife on Sundays though. Many of them spent the day preparing Sunday lunch and baking in the afternoon in readiness for Sunday tea, which was a better than average mealtime. Sunday tea usually consisted of roast beef left over from lunchtime, followed by jelly and custard and an assortment of baked items such as apple pie, custard pie, fruit loaf and 'fatty cake', made with the remnants of the pastry. This could be an even more elaborate affair whenever relatives came for tea, when a tin of salmon could be opened and a large trifle displayed in the centre of the table. This was more or less the routine from week to week for most of the people in the village, however, change was on the horizon.

Some of the villagers had already decided they had had enough of living in primitive conditions and decided to take advantage of moving into the new council houses being built outside the village. It seemed inevitable that the Hudson's would have to leave the village and move into a three bedroom council house to accommodate their mixed family who were growing up very fast. This bothered Harry. Some of his friends had already disappeared off the scene when their parents had taken advantage of moving into a new council house. But it was not compulsory, and the local authorities did not force the issue, because demand was greater than supply. In fact, some families had been on the housing list since before the war. Harry was further troubled by thoughts of what would happen to Uncle Jack if they moved out of the village. The old man had been a great influence on his life and although he was only twelve years old, Harry was becoming set in his ways. He did not relish the thought of living on an estate where all the houses looked the same and there were no 'back alleys' where you could play marbles, or hide and seek; these and other games were all played by him and his friends in the back streets of the village. His own village was surrounded by a brook which twisted and wound its way through nooks and crannies overhung by trees and bushes. It was an ideal place to go to escape from the troubles of the world. Boys of his age made rope swings across the brook or caught sticklebacks and frogs from it and even built dams across it, which held enough water for them to swim in.

Harry had been to the council estate once when one of his friends had taken him to visit relatives. He had not been impressed by what he saw and thought such a place would be very boring to live in. Besides, there appeared to be no 'corner shops'. In fact, there seemed to be no shops at all! Far different than Hindsford then, where there was a shop on every corner, three outdoor licences and five 'beer-houses'. Also, there was a full row of shops, all next to each other, on the main road leading out of the village. These shops sold anything from grocery and bakery, to clothes and shoes. So there was no need to leave the village, not unless you wanted hot running water, a bathroom, a front garden and a private backyard.

Harry's mother, wanted all of these. She was tired of struggling with her family cramped into a two up and two down, with none of these amenities. She had less time than ever now, since she was compelled to work full time in the cotton mill to help make ends meet. Uncle Jack agreed to look after her youngest child who was only two years old, and Harry and the others had to fend for themselves, especially at lunchtime when Kitty was not around. Harry was dumbstruck when his mother came home from work one evening and told him she had been to the Town Hall and had put her name on the housing list. He was quite upset about this, as things seemed to be slotting into place. He had just been given the paper delivery job, sooner than he had expected. In fact, he was not yet quite old enough in the eyes of the law to do the job, but the prospect of earning ten shillings a week was sufficient incentive for him to take the job, and hope it would not be noticed by those in authority. Harry now had a steady income, there was also extra money corning into the house, due to his mother's job. Things were looking up again, so there was certainly no need to leave the village. He was glad to learn that his father also had no wish to leave the village and live in one of the 'cardboard boxes'.

"I've seen them being built; they're nowt but 'cardboard boxes'," said his father, in one of the frequent arguments he and Kitty were having over the matter.

He would rant on about the toilet being inside the house, and say: "Who the hells idea was it to put the crap house indoors? Its place is outside at the bottom of the yard! They're a set of dirty buggers who thought of that idea! We're not going into a council house, and that's that!"

Kitty would become depressed at the thought of having to bring up her family in their present circumstances and would sometimes be reduced to tears with the whole matter. She left home on two occasions and went to live with relatives when she could no longer cope with the struggle of full time work in a cotton mill, and trying to raise a family in such conditions.

Harry was now troubled with mixed feelings. There was a good chance they would not have to leave the village because his father was totally against the idea and this suited him. On the other hand, he did not wish to see his mother cry and become depressed by being denied something that most people would take for granted. He was aware that his mother had very little pleasure in life and asked for nothing; her only concern was for the well-being of her family - this gave her the strength to carry on.

She would then become upbeat and tell him. "It all comes to them that wait."

In the Summer of 1951 the whole village was buzzing with excitement. People were stopping each other in the street to share the exciting news: The Hindsford and Atherton CO-OP Society had declared a dividend of three shillings and fourpence to the pound. It was 'Quarter Ending' week, which meant people who shopped at the CO-OP were about to be rewarded by a cash refund on their purchases over the previous twelve weeks.

Every purchase was recorded by a small ticket receipt of the amount spent. The shopper saved the receipts and stuck them onto an adhesive card, which was handed in at any of the CO-OP's shops in the area, along with their membership number. It was a welcome cash bonus for those who did their shopping at the CO-OP, especially if you had a large family and spent a considerable amount of money.

The system was not unique to the CO-OP in the village; it applied to the Co-operative movement throughout the country. The Co-operative Society had been founded in 1844 in the Lancashire cotton-spinning town of Rochdale. Northern folk were very proud of the fact that it was them who had founded a great enterprise which was now flourishing throughout the world – and the people themselves were the owners.

On this particular occasion, the villagers were proud and confident that their own local CO-OP had broken all previous records in declaring its dividend. There was talk of it being a national record throughout the whole movement; newspaper reports confirmed this by saying: 'The Hindsford and Atherton CO-OP Society has paid a record breaking dividend of three shillings and fourpence to the pound, this is the highest dividend ever to be paid throughout the whole Co-operative movement in the country'.

The dividend was usually doled out in the CO-OP hall, where several large tables were laid out with small piles of cash placed over a sheet of paper, with details of the member's share number and purchases over the previous twelve weeks. Members were invited to queue up at the row of tables and declare their share number and name, they would then be handed their cash by an official member of the CO-OP committee; these were always elderly retired men who had spent their working lives as managers, or were staunch members of the church or had held some other official capacity. They seemed to enjoy their position; perhaps it was because they had some control over the money spent by the villagers. Nevertheless, they certainly did a good job for their members by ensuring the CO-OP was well-managed and efficient, which was beneficial to the whole community.

There was always an atmosphere of optimism and high spirits on 'divi day', it meant they could enjoy a better than average weekend – with perhaps a bus ride to one of the larger towns to spend some of their extra money.

On more than one occasion, some women had asked Kitty: "How are you going to spend the 'divi' money? You must have a bob or two due to you with all the money you spend on that family."

They were usually surprised when she told them she did not shop at the CO-OP. She would point out to them they had probably seen one of her children shopping at the CO-OP, but this had been for Uncle Jack or Mrs Timperley, so 'divi day' was no big deal for the Hudson family. On this occasion it meant quite a lot to Uncle Jack, he was swelling with pride as various people told him he must he very proud that his mother had been one of the founder members of this wonderful institution. He had often tried to persuade Kitty to join the CO-OP and reap the benefits of the 'divi', but Kitty could not join without the approval of her husband and Dick Hudson certainly did not approve of joining an organisation that, in his opinion, was bordering on the edges of socialism.

Harry thought that, as Uncle Jack was in such a good mood, it would be a good time to ask him if he would show him some gold.

"O.K. then," said the old man. "Let's go an' see what we can find."

They went back into Uncle Jack's house where Harry expected him to open an old chest which he kept upstairs, but he did not. He opened one of the drawers in the sewing machine and rummaged through a pile of old buttons.

When he found what he was looking for, he threw it on the table and said: "There! That's proper gold!"

"But it's only a coin," said Harry.

"Aye. That's true. But it's real gold. It's a sovereign."

Harry admired the bright gold coin and looked at the date - 1887.

"Why does it look so new?" asked Harry.

"Because it was made to celebrate the Golden Jubilee of Queen Victoria in 1887 and some people saved them as souvenirs, so some of them did not go into circulation. I expect this was one of them. There's probably two or three more sovereigns among all these buttons. I'll sort them out sometime." With that he threw the coin back into the sewing machine drawer among the hundreds of buttons and other bric-a-brac.

Harry then pointed to a heavy, bright coloured ornament on top of the display cabinet. He had seen it many times before but had not shown any interest in it. The ornament was in the form of a horse, with its rider leaning against it as they both rested. Both man and beast were enjoying a quiet moment of peace and contentment, the horse quietly grazing whilst its rider took in the scenery of the countryside.

"Is that gold as well?" said Harry.

"No, said Uncle Jack. "It looks a bit like gold, but it is made of bronze. It is very old and was probably made in France. Anyhow young man, I think it is time for tea now and perhaps a couple of pints at the club later on. I think we can afford it out of the 'divi'."

With the excitement of 'divi day' over, the village returned to normal life, which was very much like living in the past. Its rows of terraced houses and corner shops were reminiscent of another age. Each corner shop had two or three of the stove-enamelled signs fastened to the front, advertising popular products of the day such as: 'Rowntrees Cocoa', 'Bovril', 'Oxo', 'Marmite', 'Sunlight Soap', 'Lyons Tea' and 'Bisto'. Some of the streets were still cobbled and lit by gaslight and were usually strewn with horse manure left behind by the twenty four Shire horses used by the CO-OP to transport their goods to the outlying districts.

A permanent smell hung over the village. It was a mixture of steam and smoke from the colliery, boiling pig swill from the pig farm and the large natural deposits of the CO-OP horses. Gas mantles still flickered in some houses, but this was by choice of the occupiers who had refused to have electricity installed, even at the expense of the local authority. They were elderly people who regarded electricity as dangerous, or had no use for it. Others had seized the opportunity and moved forward with the times. Nevertheless, the lifestyle of the village was worlds apart from many other parts of the country.

Harry's father, Dick and Uncle Jack had had electricity installed into their own houses in 1931, at their own expense. This had enabled them to purchase top of the range radios well before the war, when other families had to make do with a crackling old set powered by two glass bottles filled with acid. Even after the war, Harry had often been asked to carry these heavy glass bottles, called 'accumulators', to the local garage to get them recharged with electricity. This would remind him of how fortunate he was, living in a house with electricity. People would go on about his mother Kitty having an electric iron, whilst they had to make do with heating smoothing irons in the fireplace or struggling to lift pieces of red hot iron from the fire and dropping them inside a primitive 'box iron'. In reality, it was the only modern aid that made Kitty's life easier as she could get through the ironing quicker.

As the new decade gathered pace, television sets began to appear on the scene, usually purchased by people who just a few years earlier had lived in gas lit houses with no electricity, or even a radio. Some families went on holiday to the seaside for a week, or even a fortnight and one or two people actually bought motor cars. Village life, for some families, was beginning to improve at last, but life in the village for the Hudson's, would only get harder.

The family rows continued, especially when it was learned that another neighbour had decided to pack up and leave the village. Kitty would go on about Mrs 'So and So', and her family moving to a brand new council house complete with bathroom and hot water...not to mention gardens back and front. But it was no use. Dick Hudson would have none of it. He did not wish to leave a house he had lived in for more than forty years. As head of the family, he had sole rights to make this decision. Like most women of that period in time, Kitty would have to abide by it. It had often been pointed out to Kitty that Uncle Jack's house would be just the right thing for her family, why not just swap houses? Its three large bedrooms and private back yard would accommodate the whole family in much better conditions, so there would be no need to leave the village. Kitty had already realised this some years before and had occasionally discussed it with Harry and his father. It had been decided not to put Uncle Jack in an embarrassing and awkward situation by asking him to give up a house he had lived in for more than *fifty* years. Also, because the Hudson's were not members of the CO-OP, there was no chance of living in his house, so the matter was not pursued any further.

Life carried on as best it could and Kitty decided to embark on a programme of modernisation. After an evening meal, she announced to the family that she had been to the Gas Showrooms and had ordered a water heater.

"At least we will all have hot water now," she beamed. "Also, I have spent £2 on a second hand gas boiler from one of the neighbours and by this time next week, they will both be fitted and working."

"How much is the water heater?" Dick asked, slightly shocked that such a hire purchase agreement could be obtained without his signature.

"It cost £15. Two pounds deposit and five shillings a week for fifty six weeks," said Kitty.

Dick said very little but wondered what the world was coming to, when women could obtain goods without their husband's signature. However, the rest of the family were relieved that he probably approved of Kitty's actions, when he paid a handyman ten shillings to demolish the old brick-encased coal boiler.

He seemed quite pleased with himself and remarked: "There. We now have a bigger kitchen to go with our hot water heater and gas boiler."

These little improvements helped to keep the peace and deter any more talk of moving to a council house.

A WONDERFUL DECADE

Although Harry was now earning ten shillings a week for delivering newspapers, it never seemed enough money for him to purchase a bicycle. To own a bike was beyond his wildest dreams. In fact his desire was so great, he had often dreamed that someone had given him a second-hand bike, only to find himself bitterly disappointed on awakening. Yet his old friend Jimmy Collins had had *eight* bikes, besides a whole lot of other things Harry had never had... Was there no justice in the world? To make matters worse, Jimmy had appeared on the scene with a new air-gun and new top-of-the range leather 'wind-jammer', its pockets stuffed with an assortment of sweets and novelties, yet his father was still a guest in H.M. Prison Service. Once again, Harry would bitterly complain to his parents.

"How could one person have so much?"

His father's answer was usually the same.

"We all know where the stuff is coming from. It helps a lot if you have friends who live close to Liverpool Docks."

This was the case with Jimmy's older sister's many boyfriends.

Harry's mother would answer: "I have told you before, if you wait for something for long enough, it will come to you."

She would then go on to say how she had wished and hoped and waited for years for a hot water supply, and finally got it and was now waiting for a new tiled fireplace to replace the old black-leaded range. She was sure it would come to her in good time.

Harry's spirits would rise on hearing his mother's statements. He would become reasonably confident that, if he waited long enough, he would eventually own a bike. But what about the council house? What if his mother was still wishing and waiting for a council house? If this was so, then Harry worried they would eventually get one and their lives would change. Harry, like his father, did not want change – at least not in this direction. They were both prepared to have *some* kind of change, provided it did not mean leaving the village. Thoughts began to strike Harry; somehow or other they would have to live in Uncle Jack's house or at least any of the other three houses next to it – all owned by the CO-OP.

These were the only three-bedroom houses in the village apart from a row of 1930's semis which were privately owned and not available for rent. It had sometimes passed through Harry's mind that Uncle Jack would not live forever and sooner or later he would no longer be around. Who would get his house then? He would soon dismiss these thoughts, because he would rather Uncle Jack's passing would be later rather than sooner, yet something in the back of his mind kept telling him they would all live in the house at sometime in the future.

All periods in time leave behind nostalgic memories; some more than others. The 1950's would be seen as one of the most nostalgic periods in time because it still embraced an old world Victorian and Edwardian charm. It was still very much a world of terraced houses, cobbled streets, gas lamps, horses and carts, 'The Dandy' and 'The Beano' and, for 'posher' children, the newly-introduced 'Eagle' comic which peered into the future.

This decade would also signal the demise of a great power that had sustained the nation for 200 years. Steam was still the main source of power in industry and steam locomotives were still very much in charge when it came to long distance overland travel. Steam would be the most nostalgic memory left to future generations; its great reign ended at the end of a wonderful decade when the nation's Prime Minister (rightly or wrongly) kept telling his people; 'You've Never Had It So Good'.

The threat to steam locos came in the first years of the decade, with the introduction of diesel electric powered locos. The first two in service were known as 'The Deltics', and were numbered 2000 and 2001. They usually operated together as 'Double Headers'. Most train-spotters were keen to see them because they were something of a novelty. They were listed in the famous Ian Allan book and most schoolboys were eager to tick them off – Harry Hudson included.

Word had spread around the village that they would pass through the Northern town of Wigan which by now had been made famous by the writer George Orwell. The timing could not have been better: 3.40 PM on a Saturday afternoon.

Harry and his friends boarded a train for the ten mile journey to the main railway station at Wigan. They arrived early, with the intention of getting a few hours of train-spotting in, as they had done on previous occasions. They had learned from past experience that you had to travel if you wished to avoid getting 'stinkers' in your own district.

The station was crowded with hundreds of people and most of them were not passengers waiting for trains; they were a mixture of interested onlookers and train-spotting schoolboys who had more or less taken the station over, by occupying all the available platform space, for which they had paid a fee of two pence each.

The situation began to get worse as the afternoon wore on. It reached a stage where incoming and outgoing passengers had great difficulty in leaving or boarding their train. The station master appealed for order through the loudspeakers but it had little effect, as hundreds of schoolboys jostled and pushed each other for better vantage points to see the first 'Deltics" in use on Britain's Railways.

The situation became dangerous, with the possibility of someone falling off the platform and onto the track. Station staff began to act, on the announcement of the 3.05 PM non-stop express. The excited onlookers were pushed back and squeezed into any available space, away from the edge of the platform. It was a wise move and may well have prevented casualties as the 'City Of Stoke-On-Trent', a 'Stainier Class' locomotive thundered through the station at 80 mph. The station buildings shook as the great locomotive passed through amidst great excitement and cheers. The excitement did not die down, as the time of the 'Deltics' arrival began to draw near.

The station master requested the assistance of the police who quickly arrived on the scene to deal with the situation. Everyone between the ages of ten and fifteen were herded into a goods yard behind the waiting room of the station, Harry amongst them. Once again, he felt sick in the pit of his stomach; railways and policemen – he had experienced this before and was fortunate to get off with what he did. He had also been warned there would be no second chances if he landed himself in trouble again. For the next thirty minutes of his life, his interest in locomotives evaporated, as the large iron door of the goods yard was slammed shut and locked on himself and three hundred other train-spotters.

The police then disappeared, most likely to the station master's office to sup pots of tea whilst their 'prisoners' stewed in isolation; Harry wondering what his fate would be and the rest of them worrying they would not see the 'Deltics'.

After what seemed to be an eternity, the police arrived on the scene again and released their 'prisoners' from the goods yard. They were then led back to the platform which, by this time, had been cleared of most of the people awaiting trains. More space had been made available by removing porter's trucks and luggage parcels. The time on the station clock was now 3.35 PM. An officer addressed them all, telling them they would all be sent home if they did not stand still and behave themselves.

A quietness came over the station. Harry had experienced this before – it was very much like when he had waited to see the 'Royal Scot' passing through his home town. The silence was broken by the loudspeakers announcing that the 3.40 PM train for Manchester was on time and would stop to take on passengers. Harry felt quite pleased; he had not secured himself a good position amongst the three hundred and odd others but at least he would now have a better chance of seeing the 'Deltics'.

Once again, quietness descended over the station. It was broken only for a few seconds by the operating mechanism of the signals, which were now being moved to their correct position. Harry's heart began to beat faster as he could hear the sound of an approaching train; this time the sound was somewhat different... He could hear a humming and droning sound, instead of the usual 'sh-sh' of a steam locomotive, but this was still accompanied by the usual sound as the wheels of the carriages passed over the joints of the track. It was followed by the screeching sound of moving parts of iron and steel coming together as the brakes were applied to bring the train to a halt.

Suddenly, two bright blue locomotives appeared into view and, within seconds, they came to a halt. So this was the great moment then... This was what everybody had waited for...

People began to move from their places to get a closer look at the 'Deltics', but this time, under the watchful eyes of the police, there seemed to be better behaviour. Eventually Harry and a few of his friends managed to get close to the locomotives for a few minutes. During this time a few V.I.P. passengers boarded the train, whilst routine maintenance was carried out on the locos. A few local newspaper reporters took photographs and asked questions, whilst the Lord Mayor shook a few hands. Everyone was then told to stand clear as the signal was given for the train to move on.

71

As the train began to disappear into the distance, Harry began to wonder what all the fuss had been about. He was not very impressed by these 'Deltics', they were boring when compared to steam locos; they had no fire in their belly and you could not see any moving parts. Besides all this, it needed two of them to haul seven carriages – something which any class of steam loco would be able to do on its own. No! He was not impressed with the likes of numbers 2000 and 2001, especially as these locos represented a future of change, which was something he did not want.

At the start of the new school term in January 1952, Harry Hudson learned he had been relegated from form 2A to form 2B. It was something that he had been dreading. Apart from the stigma of relegation, he would now have to face change whether he liked it or not. He had been relegated along with three more boys from a class of thirty one pupils; his position in class had been number twenty eight and for a couple of days he was the subject of jibes from his former class mates. He consoled himself in the knowledge that three other boys had done worse than himself and his parents need not know until the end of June when the school report would be issued.

Within a couple of weeks he soon learned change was not all that bad, in fact, it was sometimes for the better. His new form master was Mr Buchan the Art teacher who quickly informed them all that they would be seeing more of him and less of Mr so-and-so etc. This was greeted with a few cheers because he had a reputation of being fairly easy going and his classroom was bright and pleasant because it was full of drawings and paintings done by some of the brighter pupils. However, he reminded them that, as form master, he would also be teaching them Mathematics, English, and Geography. He then went on to inform them that some things would *not* change, and they would still be taught History by Mr Morten, Woodwork by Mr Corlish, and Science by Mr Lyon. Harry was quite pleased with himself on hearing this; he was on reasonable terms with those teachers.

Mr Buchan then went on to tell them they would also be taught a new subject – Craftwork, under Mr Hodkins. A low groan came from a few pupils who had been unfortunate enough to have experienced discipline or physical punishment at the hands of this teacher. Charles Robert Hodkins was a tall, slim man who sported a pencil moustache; his hair was neatly combed backwards with a small parting and dressed with hair cream. In fact, his hairstyle could well have been used to portray the famous 'Brylcreem' adverts of the 1950's. He was a strict disciplinarian and had served in the Second World War as an R.A.F. pilot. He was fanatical about punctuality, and did not suffer fools gladly.

Harry soon settled in with his new classmates and began to feel more confident in his approach to lessons. Given the knowledge that most of his fellow pupils had always been in a B form, whereas he had had the experience of an A form, he therefore had an advantage. Life at home carried on. The eldest of Harry's two sisters had now started Senior School. and Kitty was constantly being reminded by the neighbours of how her family were growing up and how she would soon have another worker. This was all very well and life would be less of a financial struggle, but the real problem was the worsening situation of a growing mixed family living in a two up and two down with no bathroom and very little privacy.

The family arguments regarding this situation continued, especially when Kitty reminded them all that her circumstances would give her some priority on the housing list. For the time being, she began to spend her efforts on further improvements at home and decided some of the furniture had to go.

The furniture in the Hudson household was a mix-match of items ranging from the Victorian period to the late 1930's. Dick Hudson had acquired some of it from relatives of an earlier generation and, with the exception of a few items, had purchased the rest when he married Kitty. The living room of the house contained a large Victorian mahogany sideboard with three large bevelled mirrors which were richly decorated with floral scenes around the edges. Bow fronted in the centre with rich ornate carvings on the front of the drawers, it was a magnificent piece of Victorian furniture, but far too large for the house it now occupied. Kitty decided it had to go, along with the plant stand pedestal of the same period. She considered them to be 'old fashioned' and an embarrassment in these modern times.

An upright piano occupied another part of the room. It was finely veneered in walnut and proudly displayed the Royal Crest and maker's name in gold lettering under the keyboard lid: 'MAKERS BY APPOINTMENT TO H.M. THE QUEEN'. Kitty had decided this had to go as well; no one in the family could play it because they had never been taught, or were ever likely to be. However, the wooden turned candlesticks and Westminster Chime clock that rested on top of the piano could stay. These had been given to Kitty as wedding presents and were considered to be in keeping with the times.

The centre of the room was occupied by a heavy dining table, but for some strange reason it had no matching chairs. Two wooden recliners faced each other, divided by a home-made rug in front of the fireplace. An assortment of knick-knacks filled the wooden mantelpiece above the fireplace and a large black and white lithograph picture depicting bygone scenes of deer and highland cattle grazing amongst hills and streams, hung from the chimney breast immediately above. A built-in cupboard in one side of the chimney breast contained a collection of glassware, pottery and household items. Among these was an ornate earthenware teapot, much larger than an average teapot. It was glazed in black and hand painted with a pink and white floral pattern. It had been given as a wedding present to Harry's father on the occasion of his first marriage in 1915. It was claimed to be more than a hundred years old *then* and was regarded as fairly valuable. Needless to say, it was only used on special occasions and kept well out of reach of the children, on the top shelf of the cupboard. A shelf in the opposite recess of the chimney breast displayed various bric-a-brac, including two white Staffordshire pottery dogs, finely glazed and in excellent condition. A Victorian 'Chaise Longue' occupied the space beneath the front window, but it was referred to as 'the couch' or 'sofa', the word 'Chaise Longue' was unheard of. It was high on Kitty's hit list of 'getting rid of'. A very large radio stood on a purpose built table next to the piano. It was much more sophisticated than the average radio and was Dick Hudson's pride and joy. These then, were more or less the sole contents of the Hudson's front room.

The kitchen was sparsely equipped with a sink and 'slopstone', a slightly more modern version of a Victorian clothes mangle, two 'dolly tubs', a pine kitchen table with four bentwood chairs and a modern gas cooker purchased in 1935. The kitchen shelves held an assortment of pots and pans including an 'Art Deco' chrome plated reading lamp, which was used to supplement the dingy light given by a flickering gas mantle. There was no electricity in the kitchen, so Dick Hudson had wired the lamp to the power point that

74

supplied the radio in the living room so only one appliance could be used at any one time.

Coal was kept under the stairs along with other household items, including storage for vegetables. Upstairs, the front bedroom was furnished with a late 1930's bedroom suite with bakelite and chrome handles on the wardrobe, dressing table and chest of drawers. An Art Deco style electric fire was placed in front of the small cast iron fireplace in the bedroom. This electric fire was considered to be the most modern appliance in the house. An old fashioned iron bed on which two children slept was squeezed into the remaining space in the room. The back bedroom contained one bed, on which three children slept, an old plywood gramophone cabinet, minus the works, a large tin bedroom chest full of tools and an old 'Vienna Regulator' which did not work. These were the contents of the Hudson household; it was hardly a match to compare with the contents of Uncle Jack's house next door.

As the weeks went by, Harry added two more activities to his train-spotting hobby. He had been introduced to Angling by one of his friends and was beginning to enjoy this interesting pastime; visiting the many canals, mill lodges, and ponds scattered about the industrial North. He had also learned to swim and enjoyed going to the public baths once a week.

It was on one such occasion, a simple trip to the swimming baths, he would once again be landed in serious trouble with his father. He needed a towel to take with him; this would normally have been given to him by his mother, but on this occasion she was at work, so Harry decided to get one for himself. All the clean towels were neatly ironed and hung on the clothes airing rail suspended from the living room ceiling. The correct procedure was to lower the clothes rail with the rope and pulley system, which was a common fixture of most houses then. Harry had decided otherwise and placed one foot on the arm of one of the reclining chairs and the other foot on the keyboard lid of the piano. As he reached up to grab a towel, he lost his balance and put his full weight on the keyboard lid. It was enough to jolt the piano, shaking the objects placed on it, sending them crashing to the floor! The wooden candlesticks and a few other ornaments were more or less intact, with very little damage done to them; but the same could not be said for the Westminster Chime clock! Harry picked up the clock, his hands trembling with fear, and placed it on the dining table to survey the damage.

The glass fronted dial cover had been thrown open and half severed from its hinges and the wooden casing showed signs of splitting at its jointed sections. He quickly pressed them back to their original positions, which was something of an improvement, and then made a desperate attempt to re-start the clock. He opened a small door at the back of the clock and picked up the pendulum, which had been shaken loose, and re-attached it; he had seen his father do this when regulating the clock, but on this occasion the pendulum would hardly move and the clock remained silent. Harry tried several times but it was no use. Panic and fear began to grip him as he realised the clock may be broken beyond repair. It was just his luck. Why was the *clock* damaged? Why could it not be the wooden candlesticks and other ornaments instead? These were considered to be the property of his mother and the consequences would not be severe – but the clock was a different matter. Although it had been given to his parents as a wedding present, the clock was generally regarded to be the property of his father. Dick Hudson was custodian of the clock; it was he who wound it, regulated it, set its chimes and maintained it. As far as he was concerned, women were not qualified to handle such instruments.

Harry placed the clock back onto the piano along with the other ornaments, grabbed his towel and made his way to the swimming baths. He did not really enjoy his session at the baths that afternoon and confided in his friends about the predicament he was in when they questioned him about his serious mood. There was little they could do and he accepted he would have to face the music. He decided to return home when his mother was home from work, which was usually an hour before his father, if all went well.

When Kitty returned, Harry was anxiously waiting. He quickly told her of the afternoon's events in the hope she would be able to smooth over the situation. She became quite concerned about the whole matter; knowing her husband would not take lightly to his favourite time-piece being put out of action.

"I can see it happened at twenty past two this afternoon," said Kitty, as she stared at the motionless hands of the clock.

"Yes," gulped Harry, with a glimmer of hope in his voice, "But if we move the hands to twenty to six, then you will be able to say that *you* did it when you came home from work. You are always reaching for towels from the clothes rail."

Kitty managed to raise a sympathetic laugh and remarked "Yes I know, but I always lower the rail, or I stand on a chair, I never stand on the piano. You will just have to face the music and get it over and done with; but I *will* tell your father it was partly my fault for not leaving a towel out for you."

For the next hour, Harry felt like a prisoner in a condemned cell, but he resolved to take his punishment which duly came in half a dozen lashes across his backside from his father's razor strap, followed by a severe lecture and early bedtime.

The clock was not the first casualty of household goods that had suffered damage at the hands of Harry and his siblings; but up to now it was easily the most valuable. More would eventually follow, but not always at the hands of the children.

Back at school Harry was experiencing his first lesson with the dreaded Mr Hodkins, who was attempting to teach them basketwork. Most of them were aware of his reputation for doling out punishment for the slightest offence, but they had been advised by some of the older boys that there was a good side to him, especially if you could engage him in a conversation on the Second World War or you were reasonably knowledgeable about cricket. The first lesson went reasonably well, with no punishment being given to anyone, but he reminded them all that he would be making changes next week, in view of the pathetic attempts he had seen today.

Back at home that evening, Harry began to look forward to the final episode of a thrilling case of mystery and suspense… Would Dick Barton, special agent, bring the villains to justice? Dick Barton was broadcast on the radio every evening at 6.45 PM He and his faithful colleagues, Snowy and Jock were usually caught up in some exciting adventure, bringing criminals to justice. The 15 minute episodes ran for several weeks, before reaching their final exciting conclusion, which no schoolboy liked to miss out on. Harry was due to be disappointed on two occasions that evening. The first one came when his mother informed him that the radio was no longer working.

"It broke down last night when your father was listening to a boxing match," said Kitty.

"I don't believe it! Dad told me the radio was the best for miles around and it would never break down!" Harry stated hoping she was joking.

The radio was Dick Hudson's pride and joy. He had bought it at an 'Ideal Home' exhibition in Manchester in 1935. It was reputed to be one of only *six* of its kind ever to come into the British Isles and had been exhibited by the Ferguson Corporation of America and was for sale at the princely sum of £25. The makers claimed it was the most powerful domestic radio on the market, with its wavebands reaching any part of the world. Dick Hudson had been smitten by these claims and, being something of a radio enthusiast, had decided on having the best, albeit at £25 – which was three times the price of an average radio.

For the next seventeen years the radio had lived up to its name and was often a talking point amongst the neighbours who had listened to programmes from all corners of the world on it. They often re-called the occasion of the World Heavyweight Boxing Championship in August 1937, between the great American Champion Joe Louis and the British Champion Tommy Farr. It had been billed as 'the fight of the century' and people were prepared to stay up half the night listening to their crackling radios whilst the event was being transmitted by the B.B.C. Dick Hudson had proudly invited his friends and neighbours into his home, telling them they could 'have a ringside seat at the Yankee Stadium whilst the B.B.C. was warming its transmitters up'! The radio had been able to make direct contact with the American N.B.C., due to its powerful wave bands; and two earlier fights and a countdown to the big fight had been enjoyed by the listeners.

Events like these had made the radio into Dick Hudson's most prized possession, but now it was silent. Harry realised his mother was not joking about the radio being broken when she told him to make himself scarce, along with his brothers and sisters, because their father would be home from work in a few minutes and he would not be in a very good mood. Harry was now more concerned about the possibility of missing 'Dick Barton' than he was about his father's radio.

His brain suddenly clicked into gear! He could make himself scarce by going into Uncle Jack's house, where he would probably be able to listen to 'Dick Barton' as well. He told Uncle Jack about his father's broken radio and the old man agreed to his request to listen to the programme on his radio.

"What station is it on?" said Uncle Jack, as he fiddled with the controls in preparation for the start of the programme.

Harry felt quite pleased with himself as he sat comfortably in an armchair and eagerly awaited the final episode. Suddenly, Uncle Jack's front door was flung open and in walked Harry's father, still in his working clothes, followed by several neighbours. Dick Hudson quickly informed Uncle Jack that the world's greatest tenor 'Benjamino Gigli' was making a live broadcast starting at 6.45 PM

The neighbours had gone to Dick Hudson's house in the hope of hearing the world's greatest singer on a 'state of the art radio'. In view of the situation, they would now have to listen to the programme on Uncle Jack's radio. The controls of the radio were quickly switched to the correct station, just as the great tenor began to sing. Harry could not hide his disappointment as several adults enthused over the powerful and melodious tones of the great tenor, in his rendition of 'La Donna e mobile'. Harry had resigned himself to missing the entire broadcast of Dick Barton when the radio announcer told the listeners to 'sit back and enjoy the world's greatest voice'. At the end of the programme, he could not understand what all the fuss had been about, as several adults waxed lyrical and sang the praises of Benjamino Gigli, all at the expense of him missing Dick Barton.

He learned from his school friends the following day that Dick Barton and his colleagues had almost met a sticky end in their pursuit of villains, in what had been the most exciting episode ever. He was not too pleased about this, but cheered up when his father told him the radio would be repaired in a few days time.

The days passed quickly and back at school he soon found himself once again in Mr Hodkins room, where he learned that he and a number of other boys were not suitable for basketwork. Mr Hodkins informed them that, for the time being, they would be reduced to making a simple paper knife from three pieces of plastic. It was, in effect, demotion, but Harry resolved to do his best when Mr Hodkins told them they could work on their own initiative. He had heard this word 'initiative' before; Mr Corlish, the woodwork teacher, had used it in one of Harry's school reports, but on that occasion he had emphasised the lack of it when referring to his woodworking skills. Harry's father had explained it meant you have to think for yourself, and originate your own ideas. Harry decided to put this into practice when Mr Corlish gave him and some others a choice of six designs for making a teapot stand from a flat piece of wood about the size of a small plate.

Some of his fellow pupils had been over-ambitious in their choice of design and had completely ruined their wood which had to be scrapped. Harry had been well on the way to ruining his own piece of wood, before he realised there was not enough of it left to shape one of the six designs that were available to him. On that occasion, he had re-shaped his wood into the form of an octagon. It was not one of the approved designs but nevertheless he had managed to salvage something from his piece of wood. Mr Corlish had reprimanded him, along with the others, for failing to conform to any of the six designs, but then went on to commend Harry for coming up with a design of his own. With this in mind, he felt he would be able to stay on the right side of Mr Hodkins if he used his own initiative.

On a bright February day, at 11.40 A.M., Harry and his classmates were interrupted in an Art lesson with Mr Buchan, when another teacher came into the room and whispered something into his ear. After a brief conversation, the teacher left the room. Mr Buchan then told them all to stop what they were doing and stand to attention. He straightened his tie as he announced to the class: "It is with great regret that I have to tell you all that His Majesty King George VI is dead."

After pausing and staring into the air for a few minutes, he told them all to be seated and gave them a brief history of the deceased King's reign. His mood became more upbeat as he told them that the new monarch would be known as Queen Elizabeth II and she may be even become as famous as Queen Elizabeth I or, with a bit of luck, reign as long as Queen Victoria.

"Whatever the case may be," he said "I think this is the start of a wonderful decade."

UNCLE JACK'S ESTATE

The weeks quickly turned into months as the year 1952 sped by. The nation had been informed that the Coronation of the young Queen Elizabeth II would take place on June 2nd 1953. It was just another day as far as Harry Hudson was concerned, until Uncle Jack told him it would be a school holiday and they would all be given a cup, mug or some other memento to celebrate the occasion.

"It is also my birthday, so I will be able to celebrate both occasions," said Uncle Jack in a proud voice.

Uncle Jack was a traditionalist and a great believer that the country should be headed by a monarch, but he was quite sure no one would ever equal Queen Victoria.

"Coronations are very important affairs and I have seen four of them in my lifetime; I hope I will still be living to see my fifth," said the old man.

Harry did not like to hear Uncle Jack talking like that. He was quite aware the old man was not getting any younger, but he was very fit for his age, so there was no reason why he should still not be living. Nevertheless, it was a sure sign Uncle Jack recognised mortality. This was confirmed by Kitty, who had informed Harry and his father that Uncle Jack had put his affairs in order and she was to see that they were carried out when anything happened to him. In the meantime, life carried on as normal; with the occasional family row flaring up when it was revealed that yet another family had moved out of the village, into a brand new council house. It seemed the Hudson's were being left behind in life's race, as their neighbours began to book holidays at the seaside and become proud owners of television sets.

A television set was the latest status symbol in the village. In fact, it was probably the latest status symbol amongst the working classes anywhere. For the first time in living memory, cinema audiences began to drop as whole families and their friends and neighbours huddled around a tiny screen 12 inches square or even less, to watch anything that was dished up to them. Nevertheless, it was a wonderful medium – and certainly here to stay; a sure sign that the nation was rapidly discarding its post-war austerity.

1953 dawned in a mood of optimism as the nation began to look forward to a new era under a new ruler. The Prime Minister, Winston Churchill, was full of optimism for the future, which was remarkable for someone who was nearly eighty years old. On the other hand, Uncle Jack was now becoming less optimistic of the future, especially when Harry asked him if they could build another shed and increase the size of the allotment with more poultry and a fruit and vegetable patch.

His answer was: "Not at my time of life. I may not live to see the benefit from them; these we have here will see my life out."

Harry did not like Uncle Jack talking like that; especially when the old man kept telling him that the Prime Minister was actually one year older than himself. If Winston Churchill could think like that, then why couldn't he?. Back at school, Harry had also resigned himself to the fact he was probably never going to get out of a B form for the rest of his school days – which were now less than two years away. He was doing reasonably well at English and Geography, gaining top marks at History, (since David Potter had been despatched off to Grammar School), but the same could not be said for a number of other subjects.

Harry had quite recently got on the right side of Mr Hodkins for showing initiative in the design of the plastic paper knife he had been told to make; he had taken the time and trouble to file a number of tiny teeth into the first three inches of the knife blade. Mr Hodkins had been most impressed when Harry had demonstrated the cutting ability of the simple plastic blade on a thick piece of cardboard. He was even more impressed when he learned that Harry had got the idea from using the bread knife at home, which was of course, full of tiny teeth to give it a better cutting edge. To receive praise from the formidable Mr Hodkins was no mean feat; it gave Harry more self-confidence to prove himself at other lessons. He and his classmates had been told to write a composition about their favourite pastime or hobby. The task had been given to them by a new teacher called Mr Beirne, who came from the south of England. He was proving to be quite unpopular with everyone in the school and was convinced that Northern folk lacked manners and their knowledge of the English language was non-existent. He was particularly upset after visiting the local cinema the previous evening, where he had seen several pupils.

"You have no right to be in the cinema for an evening performance. You should be at home and in bed. Worse still, not a single one of you stood to attention when the National Anthem was played."

Yes, Mr Beirne had really got it in for them and told them he would be assessing them by their efforts on the composition, where he would award marks out of fifty. Harry was determined to make an impression on Mr Beirne because he did not like to see Northern folk portrayed as ignorant or less educated than others.

He decided to write all about his new found hobby of Angling, on the assumption that most of the others would be writing about Football and Cricket, which he was no good at; the rest of them would probably write about train-spotting. He new he would be in with a good chance if he wrote about train-spotting, but he would also be competing against others.

Harry was satisfied he was once again using initiative, by eliminating any competition on his chosen subject. He was well rewarded at the next English lesson when Mr Beirne declared him outright winner, with 45 marks out of a possible 50, for a fascinating account about Angling.

"The rest of you were so predictable; football, cricket, train-spotting and so forth." said Mr Beirne. "I am absolutely intrigued and amazed Hudson; Common Carp, Bronze Carp, Leather Carp, Kinsel Carp, King Carp and Mirror Carp – not to mention, Roach, Perch, Tench, Rudd, Gudgeon, Pike, Dace, Bleak and Minnow, I did not know so many species existed. Not only that, but once you have caught them, you return them back to the water and I always thought that Angling was all about catching Trout and Salmon and killing them to eat. We learn something new everyday."

Harry was now becoming quite popular with his fellow pupils and was quite content to plough through the rest of his schooldays in a B form, with the ... ction of being reasonably good at a few subjects. ... y a couple of teachers that there was a very good ... tting back into an A form for his last year at sc ... ... improved on Mathematics and Mechanical Drawing.

Harry viewed these two subjects as basically the same; each of them required you to display your calculations by statements and figures, before giving the answer. This was something that he had paid little attention to, especially when he had been at junior school.

He was exceptionally good at Mental Arithmetic and was able to give the correct answers to mathematical problems for his own age group, but this had not been good enough for his teachers at Junior School and he had sometimes been accused of copying, which was a serious offence, punishable by having to stand in a corner of the classroom, whilst the rest of the class jeered 'Copycat" at you.

Harry had received some praise and encouragement from one teacher at Senior School for his mental calculations, but had been told this was not acceptable practice; he would have to learn the correct mathematical process by displaying facts and figures. It was then he remembered the time that he used to do Mrs Timperley's errands. He had been given considerable sums of money to purchase groceries and other goods and he had never made any mistakes giving or receiving the correct sum of money. He had not had the time or inclination to be bothered looking at written statements of figures, he simply relied on his mental ability and had got through this part of his life, with very little problems.

Harry had made his mind up to steer a 'middle of the road,' course for the rest of his schooldays and would not be deflected into concentrating any extra effort into mathematics at the expense of whatever else he was good at. He was now more interested in becoming the owner of a new bicycle and in his parents becoming the owners of a television set.

The televising of the F.A. Cup Final in May 1953 and the coronation of H.M. Queen Elizabeth II in June 1953, created extra demand for television sets throughout the nation. Many people who had been thinking of buying a set, suddenly decided this was the right time and the whole nation went 'Television Crazy'. Sales of television sets in the North probably outstripped anywhere else; this was due to the All Lancashire final between Blackpool and Bolton, which would become famous as: '*The Stanley Mathews Final*'. The Spring months of 1953 were more or less the turning point, when the nation shed its post-war austerity and would long be remembered as a period of new found prosperity.

This period in time would be remembered by the Hudson's for entirely different reasons as events began to unfold. Kitty had by this time, made herself a member of the CO-OP, but only for the purpose of buying children's clothes which could be paid for over a period of 12 weeks. In effect, it was a kind of 'Hire Purchase' agreement in which you did not need your husband's signature, plus there was the possibility of some 'divi' on your purchases at the 'Quarter Ending'. However, Kitty was strictly forbidden to purchase groceries from the CO-OP, on the orders of her husband. Dick Hudson was 100% loyal when it came to buying groceries; they had to be purchased from the corner shop. The corner shop was run by a little man in a brown overall, who was known to all the villagers as 'Bobbie'. It was Bobbie who gave Dick Hudson and his family the privilege of knocking on his door for whatever items of grocery they were short of, long after the hours of business, which was usually a 12-hour day. It was Bobbie who supplied Dick Hudson with more than his fair share of 'Woodbines' at the expense of others making do with other inferior brands of cigarettes.

It was Bobbie who would make a personal visit to the Hudson's front door after the hours of daylight and produce two tins of grade one salmon from under his overall, whispering: "I've only been allocated half a dozen tins to share between all my customers."

So there was no question about it, groceries had to he purchased from Bobbie's. Kitty's action of making herself a member of the CO-OP, was the subject of gossip among some of her neighbours.

"Got her eyes on number 31, that lady has, owd John Willie is getting on a bit he won't live forever you know." etc. etc.

It was mostly women talk; the men folk were unconcerned by such matters, but some of these women were the same ones who had encouraged Kitty to 'go after number 31'. They were good neighbours, who would go out of their way to help any family in lesser circumstances than themselves, but they also resented anyone getting on too well in life. After all, Kitty had been a member of the CO-OP for just a few weeks. whilst Mrs So-and-so and others had been members for years. It never crossed their minds that Mrs So-and-so and the others were not too interested in acquiring number 31; they would rather leave the village for a new council house.

Nevertheless, they saw themselves as guardians of fairness and decency and would often raise their voices if the CO-OP did something they did not approve of – such as raising prices or purchasing equipment and more premises, at the expense of reducing the 'divi'. It was their mothers and grandmothers who had founded the CO-OP and, quite rightly, they believed they, as women, should have a say in how it was run; but at the end of the day, it was an all male committee who ran the CO-OP and it was *they* who would decide who would occupy Uncle Jack's house whenever it became vacant.

In the declining days of May 1953, Harry was becoming concerned about Uncle Jack's strange behaviour as the two of them sat talking in front of the fire. It had been a wonderful start to the Summer; the weather was exceptionally warm and people were in high spirits as they decorated the streets with bunting and 'Union Jacks' in preparation for the coronation. Blackpool had won the F.A. cup at the expense of Bolton, so in general things felt pretty good throughout Lancashire, especially with the holidays being just a few weeks away.

Harry wondered why Uncle Jack was sitting so close to the fire on such a warm day. Generally, most people in pit villages kept a coal fire going, even on warm days; it was seen as a welcome, a cheerful focal point and a place where the kettle was always on the boil in the absence of domestic facilities in the kitchen. But in Uncle Jack's house it was even more important to keep a coal fire going for the purpose of boiling potato peelings and old vegetables, which were mashed with corn meal and fed to his poultry. It was a rare occasion when two large cast iron pans could not be seen simmering away on Uncle Jack's fireplace and today was such a day. Harry noticed that Uncle Jack had removed the pans from the fire and placed them in the hearth, well before their contents were cooked.

"These pans are keeping the heat away from me and I can't see the fire properly," moaned the old man.

He then reached into his waistcoat pocket and produced two small keys and handed them to Harry. "Here, take these Harry, these are the keys to the plot, you will have to feed the hens and look after things because I am too ill."

Harry now realised Uncle Jack was a sick man, and judging from the way he had been behaving over the last few days, he was also losing his memory. The two keys he had given him were his watch key and front door key; the keys to the plot were in the same place they had been for the last 50 years – hanging from a nail in the kitchen shelf. Harry told Uncle Jack not to worry about the plot as he was now fourteen years old, and would look after things.

Back at home for the evening meal, he voiced his concern to both his parents regarding Uncle Jack's strange behaviour; but they were already aware he was a very sick man and were about to deal with the situation. When the evening meal was finished, Dick Hudson told Harry he would need him to help to get Uncle Jack's bed downstairs. This was normal practice whenever anyone was very ill, but In the case of an elderly person, it was not a good sign and was usually only considered when their life was coming to an end.

The old man was tucked up in bed and made comfortable for the night and a visit by the doctor was arranged for the following morning. The doctor's report was not very good, Kitty was told that Uncle Jack was a 'very sick man' and would need care and attention over the next few days. She decided to take a few days off work and with Harry's help, she would try to nurse the old man back to health.

Harry was now busier than he had ever been in his life; he was having to prepare poultry feed and attend to Uncle Jack's allotment, deliver newspapers, run errands, and attend school. Kitty suggested to his father that they should keep him from school for a few days, in view of the situation.

"Certainly not! Its all very good practice for him. Why, when I was his age…" said Dick Hudson.

It was very warm when Harry came home from school the following afternoon. As usual, he popped into Uncle Jack's house to prepare the poultry feed and see how the old man was getting on.

"I want you to get me a hot water bottle, I cannot get warm," said the old man.

Harry could not understand why anyone should want a hot water bottle on such a warm sunny afternoon, but if that is what Uncle Jack wanted, then he would get him one.

"How much will it cost?" said Harry, who knew that the old man was fairly thrifty and he would be in trouble if he paid too much for it.

"I don't care how much it costs, just go and get it, but make sure you go to the CO-OP for it, at least we'll get some dlvi on it," shouted the old man. "You will find a ten shilling note in my waistcoat pocket. Just do as I say, and go and get it."

Harry had never seen Uncle Jack in such a mood before. Not only that, he now appeared to be becoming reckless with his money.

Harry returned with the hot water bottle which had cost eight shillings and threepence, to which Uncle Jack replied: "Scandalous,

I don't know what the world is coming to, just stick the divi check onto the sheet behind the cupboard door."

These were the last words Harry would ever hear from Uncle Jack, as the old man was tucked into bed with his hot water bottle and made comfortable for the night.

The next day passed very much in the same way – keeping Uncle Jack warm and comfortable, but this time with the help of Harry's father who had decided the old man required the attention of an adult male. As he went to bed that evening, Harry overheard his father saying he was going to make a phone call, as Uncle Jack was now in need of professional attention.

Harry was up very early the following morning so that he could deliver his papers and tend to the poultry before going to school. When he arrived back home, his younger brothers and sisters were getting themselves ready for school whilst his mother Kitty was doing the ironing. He instantly knew something was wrong because it was not the normal procedure of her routine of housework. She reached into her apron pocket for a handkerchief to stem the flow of tears as she put one arm on his shoulders and whispered.

"Uncle Jack is dead."

There was a few moments silence, and then he felt a feeling of sadness come over him, but he did not shed any tears. He decided there and then, that the part of his life spent with Uncle Jack, was of happier times and he would dwell on this rather than be melancholy.

Kitty dried her tears and told him that Uncle Jack's condition had worsened through the night and he had been moved to the local infirmary were he had died in the early hours of the morning.

"Your father has decided to go to work because there is nothing we can do for a couple of days and I suppose you had better go and feed the poultry and get off to school; life has to go on," said Kitty as she tried to compose herself.

Harry unlocked the door to Uncle Jack's house and was met by an eerie silence as he entered the living room. Everything else was just as it had always been; it was as though nothing had happened. His eyes quickly wandered around the room, staring at all the familiar objects he had known for much of his life... What would become of them now? He began to daydream for a few minutes as he looked into the display cabinet and remembered the time when Uncle Jack had opened the Great Bible to remind him of the difference between good and evil. He was jolted back to reality by the smell of boiled potato peelings and scraps of vegetables coming from the two cast iron pans which rested on the burnt-out coals of the fireplace. He quickly realised there was little time to spare and emptied the contents of one of the pans into a bucket of corn meal and dashed off to feed the poultry.

Back at school, Harry was still in a bit of a daydream. He could not concentrate as he tried to come to terms with the loss of someone who had been quite close to him.

"Pay attention Hudson! You seem to be in a world of your own! What's the matter with you?" Mr Hodkins shouted as he stormed over to Harry's desk.

Harry quickly explained his story of Uncle Jack's demise and the old man had been an influence on his own life. He was very upset and this was the reason for his behaviour.

"Alright. Alright, I understand. You are quite right to be upset. But from what I can gather, your Uncle Jack was nearly eighty years old and had led a decent and useful life," said Mr Hodkins.

He then went on to say Harry should look upon Uncle Jack's passing as a 'celebration of a life well spent' and lead his own life in much the same way.

Harry felt some comfort and re-assurance in Mr Hodkins words, especially when he told them that he himself had lost dozens of friends and colleagues just a few years before. He then went on to tell them of his war-time experiences as a Fighter Pilot; how he had seen many of his friends shot down and killed by the German Luftwaffe.

The whole class was now enthralled as Mr Hodkins began to tell them of how he came close to losing his own life in a 'dog fight' with a *Messerschmitt 109*.

"Rat-a-tat-tat… Rat-a-tat-tat… The machine gun bullets ripped through my cockpit and some of them pierced my left leg," said Mr Hodkins as he pointed to an iron brace protruding from below his trouser leg.

"I exchanged fire, which was enough for the *'Blighter'* to change course and disappear. I was badly wounded and in need of medical attention; but glad the bullets had pierced my leg and not the fuel tank. I then turned the crippled plane around and headed back to base."

It was the kind of stuff every schoolboy read about in stories of 'Biggles' and, more recently, in the weekly comics of 'Hotspur', 'Rover', and 'Wizard'. Mr Hodkins was now something of a hero in the eyes of everyone in the classroom. Some pupils began to take advantage of his temporary deflection from an English lesson, by asking him more questions about his experiences as a pilot; some even tried to switch the subject to cricket.

"Yes laddie, Don Bradman is probably the greatest of all batsmen, but you try telling that to someone who saw Jack Hobbs play."

His mood suddenly changed.

"Hang on a minute, if I remember correctly we are supposed to be having an English lesson, but were thrown off course with Hudson and his tale of Uncle Jack... Now everybody get back to what they were doing."

The silence as everyone got back to their work, was eventually broken by a knock on the classroom door. Mr Hodkins answered the door and engaged in a conversation with another teacher, leaving the door slightly ajar while the two of them stood in the adjoining corridor, just outside the classroom. Most of the class saw this as an opportunity to engage in a few moments of chit-chat whilst Mr Hodkins' back was turned.

Two boys hastily folded sheets of paper torn from their exercise books into paper aeroplanes and launched them into the air.

"Rat-a-tat-tat. Rat-a-tat-tat," they shouted, as they tried to enact the story they had heard a few minutes ago.

Their handiwork with modelling paper aeroplanes was good, as they remained in the air for quite a few seconds, which was enough time for Mr Hodkins, who had just finished his conversation, to see them landing close to his own desk as he stepped back into the classroom.

"Who are the boys who are responsible for this nonsense?" he bellowed.

As expected, there was complete silence. Of course, almost everyone in the classroom could provide him with the names of the culprits, but this would be 'snitching''; even Mr Hodkins would not approve of that.

"Very well then, I shall take a calculated risk of punishing the guilty offenders," said Mr Hodkins, as he surveyed the paper missiles resting at the foot of his desk. "I would assume these missiles were launched from the back two rows of desks, probably from the right hand side of the room, judging from their flight path and present position."

Everyone now thought Mr Hodkins would treat the matter light-heartedly, until he looked at the rows of canes which were used in his Basket-weaving and Craft lessons. He seemed to take pleasure in selecting one to administer punishment. He finally chose a slender cane, which was quite flexible as he swished it through the air to get the feel of it.

"Right! Starting with the back row from my left, come out one at a time," he shouted.

'Swish, swish, swish'... 'swish, swish, swish'... The first victim grimaced as he looked at three red stripes on either hand as he walked back to his place. Harry was sitting in the centre of the second row and thought he may be excused punishment – but no such luck. Mr Hodkins dealt with the whole two rows in the space of a few minutes. Fortunately for everyone, it was the last lesson of the day, so they could all go home and nurse their painful fingers... and re-assess their opinion of Mr Hodkins.

Back at home, arrangements were being made for Uncle Jack's funeral; the village undertaker had been invited to call at Uncle Jack's house, where he was met by Harry's parents.

James Edward Pendleton was a little man in his sixties, barely five feet tall. He always seemed to be permanently dressed in 'bib and brace' overalls and a white dress shirt with a starched upturned collar. He was a joiner by trade, but the sign above his premises indicated he was a very enterprising man indeed:

JAMES E. PENDLETON – JOINER, BUILDER, & CABINET MAKER, COMPLETE FUNERAL DIRECTOR, LICENSED TO SELL GROCERY, ALE, PORTER, & TOBACCO.

He was affectionately known as 'Teddy' to everyone in the village; he was the man you sent for if your roof was leaking or your window was broken. When he was not doing this, he was busy in his workshop, making coffins. Whenever the need arose, he would take off his overalls and put on his tall hat and tails (without the need to change his shirt) and officiate at a funeral. Needless to say, his wife, whom he barely ever saw, ran the grocery side of the business.

On entering Uncle Jack's house to discuss the funeral arrangements, Mr Pendleton immediately walked over to the display cabinet and ran his hands over the highly polished woodwork.

"Well, well, I remember making this donkey's years ago. It was made from an old pipe organ that used to belong to his parents."

Dick Hudson knew the story and nodded his approval.

"There's some good stuff in this house. What are you going to do with it?" said Mr Pendleton.

"Well, I suppose it will have to be sold off. My wife has been appointed to carry out his affairs," said Dick Hudson as he looked at Kitty.

"Well make sure you get a good price for everything, took me quite a while to make that cabinet you know," Mr Pendleton replied. "Now then, do you have a specific date in mind?" he asked as he opened a small notebook.

Kitty had part of her mind on the Coronation Festivities on the 2nd of June and wished to do her share of helping out amongst the neighbours.

"Could we have the funeral on the 1st of June?" said Kitty.

"Well it's a bit tight, but I think I can just about manage it because I don't think there will be much going on in my line of business the following day... Coronation, you know. Now then, Atherton or Tyldesley?" Mr Pendleton said, referring to the place of burial.

"Neither" said Kitty, "his wishes were to be buried in the same place as Jean, which was Bolton."

"Ah, I remember Jean. She was his 'live in lady' wasn't she? Anyhow, that will be O.K. but it will cost a bob or two extra you know," Mr Pendleton added as he finalised the details.

On the 1st of June, Uncle Jack was brought back to his house a few hours before the time of his funeral and laid out in an open coffin resting on two trestles beneath the front room window. As was customary, anyone was allowed into the house to pay their last respects to the deceased. It also gave some of the villagers the chance to cast their eyes around the house and pick out an item of furniture which they knew would shortly be coming up for sale. Uncle Jack's old friend, Bill Underwood, came to pay his respects. Tears rolled down his eyes as he removed his flat cap and leaned over the coffin, patting his friends face.

He said: "Goodbye John Willie, I reckon I'll soon be seeing you," then turned to Kitty and asked: "What are you going to do with his watch? Its a chronograph you know – best watch for miles around."

"I don't know," said Kitty, "I don't even know where it is. You will have to see my husband about things like that."

Uncle Jack's funeral was a small affair. Apart from a clergyman and a couple of attendants, there were just Harry's parents and Mr and Mrs Morrison who lived at Number 29.

The Morrison's were a childless couple and were referred to as Uncle Walter and Aunt Rose. Aunt Rose had done small household jobs for Uncle Jack, but nothing on the same scale Kitty had. Nevertheless, she was also a beneficiary in his will. Harry was kept away from school, but not allowed to go to the funeral. His job was to look after his younger siblings when school was out, with the help of old Mrs Timperley who had been asked to keep an eye on things.

That evening, with Uncle Jack laid to rest, Kitty and family turned their thoughts to the following day. Coronation day was a bit of a damp affair and alternative plans had to be put into action to avoid the showers. What would normally have been a street party took place in the village hall; others took place in people's homes, or any other place where there was sufficient shelter.

On the whole, the event went quite well; it gave the villagers the chance to meet up with each other and pass the time of day. A few of them expressed their condolences to Kitty and then went on to say: "Let us know when any of John Willie's stuff goes up for sale."

Things returned to normal for a couple of days, until a visitor from the CO-OP called and wished to know when Uncle Jack's house could be vacated.

Dick Hudson was spurred into action when he learned that the rent would still have to be paid – albeit on an empty house.

"Cheeky buggers! John Willie's barely cold in his grave! Do they know there would probably be no CO-OP but for the likes of his mother?" He muttered: "I'll clear the bloody house out by Friday."

The following day, Kitty received a letter naming her as chief executrix of Uncle Jack's will. She was told she could take 'Immediate Charge' and keep or sell any of the deceased's effects and would receive a final statement of the will in due course. Dick lost no time in informing the neighbours it would be 'Open House' at No. 31 a week on Friday.

The day finally came and Uncle Jack's house was open to the neighbours at 7 P.M. on a fine Summer evening. Dick Hudson had chosen Friday because it was the day when everyone received their wages, therefore they were likely to have money to spend. One by one, the neighbours politely knocked on the already open door of the house before entering. Once inside, they exchanged a few pleasantries before making their way through the house – upstairs and down, to view its contents. By about 7.30 P.M. there were about twenty people gathered in the front room, with a few spread about the rest of the house. Dick Hudson stood behind the large dining table in the centre of the room with his back to the fireplace, whilst Kitty sat on a chair at his side. Within reach was an enamel dish, a pencil and a notebook which had been placed on the table. Harry was allowed to be present, but this was to help out with moving things and showing people around. Apart from that, no other children were present.

At 7. 45 P.M. Dick rapped on the table with a large heavy soup spoon and began to speak in a loud, clear voice.

"I shall call this house to order whilst we dispose of the late Mr Howell's effects."

He was in his element; he was doing something he knew he would be good at. It was something he had always wanted to do since he had first visited the auction houses on Blackpool sea front to watch shady characters dispose of dodgy household goods to a gullible public.

There was a polite silence as he began to speak. "I think we will dispose of the larger items first and we will start with the large bevelled mirror Art Deco oak sideboard behind you. I must tell you that young Agnes Timperley has offered three pounds ten shillings for it. As some of you may know, she is getting married shortly and it will be a good start for her."

There was a mixture of polite applause and disappointment on hearing this. Agnes, who was not at the sale, was the only girl in the Timperley household and she was anxious to get away from her quarrelling bachelor brothers. There was a few moments of silence as Dick fixed his eyes on everyone in the room; it was as though he was telling them *not* to increase their offers.

He knew he could probably get a better price for the sideboard, from at least two or three people, but he smiled as he said, "Sold! To Agnes Timperley for three pounds ten shillings."

"What about the ornaments on the sideboard, are they included too?"

"No, they are not; but if anyone is interested... then make me an offer. How about two quid for the lot?" said Dick.

The ornaments in question were the carved lizards, snakes and crocodiles which had been brought back from South Africa by Aunt Jean who had spent much of her time there. She had returned home to England after her husband, who was the manager of a diamond mine, was killed in an underground accident.

"Uncle Jack told me they are made of ivory," piped Harry.

"Be quiet and go home for a few minutes and see if everything is O.K.; and make sure the youngest are getting ready for bed," said Kitty.

Harry did as he was told and went next door.

"No one interested in the ornaments, not even for a pound?" Dick said.

There was still silence; things of foreign origin did not arouse much interest amongst them and the claim of them being made of ivory was viewed with scepticism in view of the many mutations that were being sold at the time.

"Very well then, I will make a gift to Agnes and throw them in with the sideboard."

"How much will you take for this wickerwork chair I am sat on?" Dick was interrupted by a young woman who had made herself comfortable on a chair that had been brought downstairs for such a purpose.

"That, my dear, is a genuine 'Lloyd Loom' ladies bedroom chair and is part of the bedroom suite which we have not got around to yet," said Dick.

"I will give you seven and six for it," said the woman, who seemed unconcerned about the brand name.

"Could you make that ten bob?" Dick asked.

The woman shook her head as he cast his eyes around the room in the hope of attracting a bid of ten shillings. Once again there was silence; there seemed to be a politeness amongst them; they did not want to bid against each other.

"Very well then my dear, the chair is yours," said Dick, as he held out his hand to receive three half crowns, which he threw into the enamel dish whilst Kitty recorded the sale in her notebook.

"Now then… we will try to make a bit of room," said Dick as he pointed to his next item for sale.

"Will someone make me a reasonable offer for the 'Singer' sewing machine? It's getting on a bit, but it was top of the range when it was made and is still in good working order, as this young lady will vouch for," added Dick pointing to the woman who had just bought the chair.

The woman smiled and nodded her approval and stated Uncle Jack had allowed her to use the machine when she had not possessed one of her own.

With confirmation that the machine was in good working order, the first offer of seven shillings and sixpence was put forward.

"Oh come on now, we can do better than that," said Dick, who was anxious to see some paper money change hands. After all, the last item had been seven and six and he did not want to become involved in a 'small change' sale. After a bit of disheartening silence, a further bid of ten shillings was put forward.

This was a welcome relief for him. At least it was a sign of competition.

"Fifteen shillings," came an immediate reply from a woman who was accompanied by her two teenage sons.

This bid was met with cautious silence; several women set eyes on the latest bidder whose determined look put them off from bidding against her.

Dick looked around the room in the hope it would develop into an inflationary bidding match. But no such luck, as everyone in the room remained silent.

"Very well then… the sewing machine, including its accessories, buttons, needles, thread, etc. is sold to Mrs Henderson." said Dick, as he rapped his soup spoon on the table to close the sale.

After parting with her fifteen shillings, Mrs Henderson instructed her two sons to lift the heavy cast iron machine and carry it home. She followed closely behind, encouraging them to keep going as they struggled with their heavy load.

Uncle Jack's 'Murphy' radio was the next item on the agenda. It attracted several bids when Dick described it as the 'second best radio in the village'. It was sold for three pounds to a neighbour who said he had heard the radio from his own house for the last ten years because 'John Willie always had it on at full volume'. Dick was interrupted again before he could get on to his next item.

"Yes Madam, you can have the copper kettle on the fireplace hob... if nobody out-bids you. By the way, that kettle is older than John Willie himself, so make me a good offer will you?"

"Five shillings," came the reply.

"Ten shillings," shouted someone else.

This was an inflationary bid, which was what Dick wanted.

"Twelve shillings and sixpence," said the original bidder.

"Fifteen shillings," replied the second bidder.

This was followed by silence. Dick was reasonably satisfied with the last bid of fifteen shillings; he looked at the original bidder who, with a look of determination upon her face, was clearly not going to he outdone.

"One pound," she blurted out, which was sufficient to silence the second bidder.

Once again there was silence as the woman looked around the room, hoping the contest was over. Dick reached for his soup spoon and was just about to bang it on the table to close the sale, when he was interrupted.

"Did I hear you say the kettle was older than John Willie himself?" asked an elderly, well dressed man.

"Yes. It used to belong to his mother... and possibly her mother too," Dick spoke in a tone of voice which was meant to add a few more years to the kettle's age.

"In that case, I will give you one pound five shillings for it," said the man.

This was responded to by the original bidder, and the two of them began to slug it out in multiples of five shillings until the kettle's value reached two pounds ten shillings, much to Dick's delight. The original bidder eventually secured the sale after parting with two pounds fifteen shillings.

Harry returned to the house just as his father was about to start on the next item for sale. His jaw dropped when he noticed the empty space where the sewing machine had been. He suddenly remembered the gold sovereign Uncle Jack had kept in one of the drawers, amongst the buttons, needles and thread. Why did he not think to tell his parents about it? More so, there may well have been other gold sovereigns there – as Uncle Jack had indicated. He felt worried and tormented; what should he do? Tell his parents, or keep quiet about the whole affair.

After a few minutes deliberation, (in which time Dick had completed the sale of some pottery), Harry could no longer contain his guilty secret. He held up his hand to attract his father's attention.

"Can't you see I am busy… speak to me later," said Dick.

Harry felt very frustrated as his father continued with the business of selling two fireside chairs rather than listen to what he had to say. He crept around the table and whispered his story to his mother, who did likewise into Dick's ear.

Dick immediately broke off from what he was doing and spoke to everyone in the room. "I did promise you some bargains at this sale folks… well, believe you me, Mrs Henderson has just had the bargain of a lifetime! I am not going into details, but there's probably some bloody expensive 'buttons" amongst the needles and thread in the sewing machine drawers."

Everyone in the house was slightly bemused, but they did not question it further; they were eager to get on with the sale and get a bargain themselves. Kitty suggested they suspend the sale for a few minutes while one of them went round to the Henderson's to discuss the situation.

Dick refused and pointed out that he had, sold the machine, complete with accessories and it was the Henderson's good fortune when they looked into the machine's drawers. He shrugged his shoulders as he began to continue the sale.

"Win some, lose some. Right ladies and gentlemen, what about the display cabinet and its contents?"

Several hands went up at the same time, but their owners indicated they were interested in different items *within* the cabinet and did not wish to purchase a job lot.

"Very well. We will deal with the contents separately. First of all, we will try to get rid of this heavy lump of metal on top of the cabinet. Is anyone interested in the cast bronze of the 'Boy and Horse'? It is stamped on the bottom as being made in Paris."

Ten shillings was the only bid put forward; by a man who said he could use it as a 'doorstop'. The rest of them muttered that such things were out of date and they preferred china or porcelain.

"Very well then. Sold for ten shillings," said Dick.

Harry began to get *very* interested, as his father was about to dispose of the rest of the contents of the cabinet. What would become of the 'Great Bible' and 'Pilgrims Progress'?

He cast his eyes around the room as his father sold some of the hand painted pottery for just a few shillings. He noticed the old man who played a concertina to dozens of wild birds, he kept in his house, was there; two elderly ladies who did not live in the village, smiled at him. He had seen them before and remembered their names as 'Aunt Winnie', and 'Aunt Minnie'.

Dick completed the sale of the last of the pottery in the cabinet for just a few more shillings and turned his attention to the books.

"We have here a collection of books; including a Family Bible. They have been in John Willie's family for the best part of a hundred and fifty years; is anyone interested – all or part?" Dick asked.

There was complete silence all around the room; most of them had little interest in books; having been brought up to a culture of hard physical work, they spent what little leisure time they had listening to the radio or going to the cinema. However, Aunt Winnie and Aunt Minnie had been brought up in different surroundings. The two spinster sisters had had a good education, although both were now retired; Winnie had been a schoolteacher and Minnie a librarian. As sisters of Aunt Rose, the other benefactor in Uncle Jack's will, they had visited his house on a number of occasions and were probably familiar with his collection of books – *and* their value.

The sisters could hardly believe their luck as they looked around the room for any signs of interest from anyone else, before placing their bid. Winnie, the eldest and more dominant of the sisters spoke first.

"We will give you five shillings for the Family Bible and keep it for sentimental reasons, as it seems no one else wants it and it has nowhere else to go." Winnie implied she was being generous in saving the book from being thrown away.

Dick was not over-impressed, but accepted her offer, as Minnie began to whisper into her elder sister's ear.

"What do you say to ten shillings for the rest of the books?" Winnie suggested.

"Make it a pound and I will throw in 'Pilgrims Progress'," said Dick.

The two sisters were slightly disappointed on hearing this, as they fully expected 'Pilgrims Progress' would not be singled out; but they were nobody's fool when it came to knowing the value of books and they parted with their money into Dick's outstretched hand.

Dick was glad to see the back of the contents of the display cabinet and was unaware he had sold them for a mere fraction of their value.

"Now then, will anyone give me ten shillings for the display cabinet?"

Several bids followed and the cabinet was eventually sold for one pound five shillings. Harry had noticed that the elderly man who played the concertina to his collection of wild birds had shown little interest in the sale up until now. He held his hand up and interrupted Dick, who was in the process of selling the contents of the kitchen.

"Will the concertina be coming up for sale?"

"I didn't know he had a concertina. I have known him for forty years and never seen or heard of one," said Dick, who looked slightly bemused.

"Oh yes. He has one... it used to belong to his father who was quite good at playing it," said the elderly man.

"Well it is probably upstairs somewhere, but I have not got around to dealing with those items yet. We will see if it can be found." Dick added.

Harry was sent upstairs to search for the concertina, which he found in an old chest under the bed. The instrument was in a highly polished mahogany box and appeared to be in good condition, which was rather surprising, having not been played for more than forty years.

Harry was a little disappointed not to find much else in the chest apart from a few old photo frames and a pair of opera glasses. It would have been much more exciting if he had found a hoard of gold sovereigns, which he believed Uncle Jack had stashed away somewhere. He took the box and its contents and handed them to his father.

Dick lifted the concertina from its box by one of its leather handle straps, causing the instrument to inflate its bellows and give off a melodious tone.

"Does anyone know the value of these things?" he enquired.

Nobody seemed to know except possibly the intended buyer, who certainly wasn't going to say anything.

"Someone make me an offer," said Dick, who now wanted to move on and clear the house of its contents.

"Ten shillings," said the elderly concertina player, who was unopposed - mainly out of politeness, lack of interest and due to the fact that it was he who had brought it to light.

"Done!" Dick replied as he held out his hand to receive the money.

"Let me try it first," said the old man.

He picked up the concertina and handled it very gently for a few seconds before nodding his approval and satisfaction. He then proceeded to play a fast 'Jig', followed by a 'Sea Shanty', to the delight and amusement of those around him. Harry was instantly reminded of the time he had spent watching the wild birds fluttering about the old man's house, to the tunes of a concertina. The instrument now being played seemed much louder and more melodious than the one he had heard then. The old man completed his medley of tunes and was applauded by everyone in the house – with a few shouts of 'Encore!' added. He smiled as he packed the instrument into its box, handed Dick a ten shilling note, bade goodbye to everyone and went on his way.

"Well now... after that musical recital we'll start to clear the kitchen out," said Dick, who seemed cheered and amused by the whole affair.

Most of the kitchen items were quickly disposed of; the most valuable piece was a mid-nineteenth century dresser, which was sold for the least money – five shillings. The contents of the front bedroom were also sold very quickly; most of the furniture consisted of a walnut veneered bedroom suite in Art Deco style. A few people expressed their surprise at Uncle Jack possessing such 'modern things', only to be told that this furniture had been bought by Aunt Jean from the most expensive store in Bolton.

The rest of Uncle Jack's furniture had been consigned to the two back bedrooms and was no longer in use. Dick sold the Art Deco bedroom suite for the princely sum of seven pounds ten shillings, along with a few silver photo frames and a 'Clarice Cliff' water jug, which he threw in for good measure. The only old item in the front bedroom was a 'Vienna Regulator' which hung on the wall where it could be seen by anyone lying in bed. Dick was offered one pound for the late nineteenth century mahogany cased wall clock; he was reluctant to sell at this price, until it was pointed out to him that the clock was incomplete. The potential buyer pointed to the ornate pediment which adorned the top of the clock case. The left hand and middle pediments were topped with finely turned finials, but the right hand finial was missing. It had clearly been broken off and would be difficult to replace. In view of this, Dick agreed to the sale and was pleased when the buyer offered a further ten shillings for an unsold odd chair downstairs. The chair was the only one in the house that Uncle Jack used to sit on whilst having his meals. There were other dining chairs, but he never used them and had occasionally mentioned to Harry that this chair was well over a hundred years old.

The seat was made of woven straw, which was in remarkable condition considering its age, but the middle was devoid of varnish after a century of back rubbing, with a large, distinctive knot exposed. After a demonstration ensuring the wall clock was in working order, the buyer handed over his thirty shillings.

This more or less completed the sale of the contents of Uncle Jack's house, with the exception of some unwanted bric-a-brac and some furniture in the back bedrooms which was considered to be ugly and old fashioned. The neighbours gradually made their way from the house, some of them carrying their purchases, whilst others made arrangements to move heavy furniture at a later date.

"I reckon that's a good nights work and we've done alright," said Dick, with a contented smile on his face as they turned out the lights and locked up the house.

Back at home, the rest of the children were put to bed, whilst Harry and his parents discussed the results of the sale. Harry expressed his disappointment at the concertina having been sold; he had grown fond of its merry tunes when its new owner had played it, and perhaps he could have learned to do the same. Dick explained to him that everything from Uncle Jack's estate, that could be sold, had to be, to help pay for his funeral expenses.

"Well what about these?" Harry asked as he removed the opera glasses from his pocket. "I forgot to put them on the table alongside the concertina. Could we have sold them?"

"Yes, I am sure we could, but you might as well keep them for yourself now, as we have more important things to deal with." Dick replied.

The following morning, after he had finished his paper round, Harry was told by his mother to go and help his father to get rid of the old fashioned furniture left unsold in Uncle Jack's back bedrooms.

This consisted of a mid-nineteenth century mahogany bow-fronted chest of drawers, a Regency 'tallboy', a military chest and two Victorian easy chairs.

"We are not struggling to get these downstairs, they are too heavy, besides that, nobody wants them, so we will break them up and use them for firewood," said Dick.

The two of them set about the furniture with a saw, a hammer and an axe. In the space of two hours, the most valuable contents of Uncle Jack's house were reduced to firewood.

Within the next few days the house was empty, as the last of the furniture was removed and carried away on hand-carts by its new owners. Harry felt very sad as he watched his parents make a final inspection of the house. Every movement, or even the slightest sound of someone talking, was amplified into an eerie hollow sound which reverberated through the house. There were no embers in the fireplace and even the smell of boiled potato peelings and poultry feed had disappeared.

Uncle Jack's pipe and tobacco pouch lay forlornly on the fireplace hearth in exactly the same place he had left them. As the three of them made their way to the front door, they stopped and remained silent, each of them looking around the room in quiet contemplation. They remembered happier times and wondered if such times would ever return and when? Finally, Dick reached up and turned out the lights, removed the heavy key from inside the house door and the three of them stepped outside. The key was re-inserted on the outside and the house was secured until the arrival of its next occupants.

The next few days saw a period of normality return to the Hudson household. The Summer holidays were only a few days away and, back at school, Harry struggled through the exams which would determine his final year at school. In the meantime. Kitty made a half-hearted attempt to see if it was possible to become the next tenant of Uncle Jack's house. She made her enquiries when an official from the CO-OP called round to collect the on-going rent which she was obliged to pay as custodian of Uncle Jack's Estate. Although she half expected what the answer would be, she was disappointed to learn that the house was going to be let to a milk round man employed by them. Dick was even more upset when he learned this would not take place for a few weeks, during which time the rent would still have to be paid.

Kitty consoled herself with the fact she was the main beneficiary in Uncle Jack's will, which was now in the final stages of being wound up. She had decided if she could not have Uncle Jack's house, then she would do her best to improve her own house. She surprised them all by saying she had ordered a new tiled fireplace at a cost of £14.

Harry was even more surprised when she handed him £2 to place as a deposit on a brand new bicycle, saying: "I've told you before…it all comes to those who wait."

Kitty's little legacy which would allow her to do these things, or 'go on a spending spree' as Dick called it, was confirmed by a solicitor's letter which arrived a few days later.

The letter contained a typewritten statement headed:

THE ESTATE OF JOHN WILLIAM HOWELL, deceased
EXECUTRIXES DISTRIBUTION ACCOUNT

INCOME	£		
Cash in the house	3	17	5
Men's Society Benefit Paid	12	10	0
Hindsford & Atherton CO-OP Society Shares dividend	7	8	9
Life Policy Claim	17	9	7
Insurance Policy	25	3	9
Co-0p Savings Bank.	72	13	9
National Coal Board Pension.		3	0
Household Furniture, Personal Effects, Poultry & Sheds	50	0	0
TOTAL	189	16	3

EXPENDITURE			
Furniture, Personal Effects, Poultry and Sheds	50	0	0
Floral Wreath	2	5	0
Death Certificates		14	0
Bus Fares		4	6
Telephone Calls		1	6
Men's Society Subscriptions Paid		4	10
Washing		11	0
Six Weeks rent @ 9/10 per week	2	19	0
Inscription on Tombstone	4	15	0
Half years rent for Poultry Run		3	6
James E. Pendleton Funeral Expenses	33	0	0
Mr. Richard Hudson Expenses for nursing deceased	16	4	5
Bank Charges		10	6
Solicitor's Costs, Charges and Expenses of Probate and Winding Up	20	15	0
Carried Forward	132	18	5
BALANCE	56	17	10

To be divided as follows:

Catherine Hudson: ¾ share   £42   13   4
Rose Morrison: ¼ share £14   4   6

Kitty was more than pleased after reading the statement; she had never seen such sums of money in all her life. At last, her boat had come in! Dick was not quite so happy with the statement and thought Mr Pendleton had 'overdone it a bit' with the funeral charges.

"I know he provided one of his best elm coffins, with brass finishes and two limousines, but he's certainly made us pay for it. I also notice the solicitor has had his ten pennyworth, they're a law unto themselves them buggers are."

He calmed down when he realised the solicitor had actually done them a favour by valuing Uncle Jack's furniture and personal effects at just £50. Anything that could be raised above this sum was entirely due to their efforts and they did not need to disclose it.

No one ever really got to know what the sale of the furniture and personal effects *actually* raised in terms of cash, except Dick, who was now beginning to feel pleased with himself about the way he had handled the whole affair.

A footnote in the solicitor's statement informed Kitty that she had the authority to collect the money from his office whenever she wished. She and Harry made a trip to collect it from the given address, which incidentally was quite close to the cycle shop – where a brand new 'Hercules' bicycle was also waiting to be collected... The pair of them walked home that afternoon, happy and content, their dreams having been fulfilled, thanks to Uncle Jack's Estate.

LIFE GOES ON

As the long Summer days began to wind their way through the month of July 1953, Harry began to think this was surely the happiest time of all his life. There were five whole weeks ahead of him, during which he and his friends need not bother about school. This enabled him to take full advantage of his new bicycle, by going on long rides in the countryside and finding hidden railway tracks, in the hope of spotting a rare 'namer'. What better way to spend the time, than to pack some sandwiches and a bottle of water into the saddlebag, with fishing tackle tied to the cross-bar and head for a secret pond way out in the countryside. Yes, his new bike had certainly improved his lifestyle; so much that he began to treat it like a piece of fine porcelain. The gleaming blue and yellow 'Hercules' was his pride and joy. It was cleaned and oiled almost everyday and completely dried off with rags whenever it had been out in wet weather. He had waited all his life for it and nothing or no one was going to damage it or take it from him; it was his greatest possession.

But there was just one drawback... the bicycle was becoming a burden on his resources. The weekly payments of eight shillings and sixpence, to pay off the remaining balance of twelve pounds, left him with only one shilling and sixpence from the ten shillings he received for delivering newspapers. This was barely the same amount of money he had earned when he was doing Mrs Timperley's errands.

Something had to be done; but what?. There was no question of him parting with his bike! There had to be some other way of earning some extra money, at least in the short term. He had learned from experience, problems usually sorted themselves out in the long term. It occurred to him that there were large piles of firewood available to him, in the form of Regency and Victorian furniture, recently broken up by him and his father. He quickly transformed the rough and broken pieces into thin, even sticks neatly tied in bundles, which were slightly larger than those available in the local shops.

This generated a little extra income for a few weeks as he trudged through the village in his spare time, selling (Regency) firewood at threepence a bundle. Kitty was aware of Harry's difficulties in maintaining the weekly payments on his bike and promised to 'chip in' whenever she could. There was also another slight problem which needed to be dealt with.

Dick had been recently commenting on the low egg production coming from Uncle Jack's poultry. As Harry was now in charge of the allotment, Dick thought *he* should do something about it.

"Fourteen eggs a day is not good enough from two dozen hens. They're not earning their keep and you should be thinking of killing off some of the older birds," said Dick.

Harry was horrified! He had seen Uncle Jack do this when some of the birds had become a liability because of their age. It was a nasty experience in which the unfortunate creature's neck was wrung until it lay lifeless, which took some considerable time – and a strong pair of wrists. No! There was no way he could this dastardly deed; he just hoped the egg production would rise and the guilty offenders would go unnoticed and die of old age. In the meantime he tried to economise with the preparation of the poultry feed, which was now being made on Kitty's kitchen stove (which she was none too pleased about).

The Summer holiday passed all too quickly and Harry began to think about the new school term. Life seemed to go on in very much the same way for the Hudson's, but elsewhere in the village, there seemed to be a degree of change.

The first 'Ford Populars' and 'Morris Minors' began to appear. Their proud owners cleaned and polished them on Sunday mornings and set out with a 'Thermos' flask and sandwiches in the afternoon; their destinations being such 'distant places' as Chester, Blackpool, Southport and Morecambe, or perhaps a visit to 'Aunt Gladys' and 'Uncle Sid', to show off their new motor . They were usually home before the hours of darkness, when the vehicle would be locked up in an asbestos garage and not used until the following weekend.

What used to be a day at the seaside had now become a week for many families. Blackpool was still the main choice, but for the better off, Devon or Cornwall, or even, the rare exception, Ostend or the Austrian Tyrol. There really was a feeling of optimism and prosperity, as predicted by one of Harry's teachers when he referred to it as 'A wonderful Decade'.

Harry and his siblings had never had a holiday away from home; and it would be quite a while yet before any of them would have the experience.

At the start of the new school term in August, Harry was not surprised to learn that he had failed to get into form 4A for what would be his final year at school. Form 4A was the highest grade in secondary education and was sufficient enough to impress most employers to offer a job in a skilled trade. However, he was pleasantly surprised to see his old pal Jimmy Collins had been promoted from the dreaded C Group and was now sitting quite close to him in Form 4B. When the surprise wore off, he became a little despondent and began to think of himself as a failure. He had started Senior School in an A Form and Jimmy had started in a C Form; now they were both in the same class... how could this be? He soon put the matter behind him when he realised Jimmy must have put more effort into gaining promotion than *he* had done to avoid demotion!

He began to feel glad Jimmy had improved his situation; it was something of an achievement for someone who could barely read in Junior School.

Kitty had come to terms with the fact that she and her family had very little chance of ever occupying Uncle Jack's house as she welcomed her new neighbours into number 31. She became quite friendly with the new lady of the house and confided that it had been her greatest wish for her and her family to live in the house.

"Well perhaps you will one day, you never know how things turn out; and it all comes to those that wait," said the new occupant.

Kitty laughed at this, it was echoing her own sentiments and repeating her own statements; she just hoped it would become a reality.

Occasionally she would get upset when any of the neighbours said things such as: "Its not right for a family of two adults and just one child should be living in a fine big house like that."

Or: "I don't think you tried hard enough Kitty; you should have moved into the house and stood the consequences."

She consoled herself by making little improvements to her own house... and listening to the recent gossip - that two families who had left the village a few months earlier, were now returning because they were unable to adapt to life on a council estate.

On hearing this latest news, Kitty greeted it with: "What goes around, comes around." She followed this up with: "It all comes to those that wait," as she showed of her newly-installed tiled fireplace to the neighbours.

As 1953 quickly wound its way out, the pace of change in the village began to move faster. The metal stove enamelled signs that were fastened to the walls of corner shops, began to be replaced by sheets of plastic advertising new and wonderful products, endorsed by trendy, modern logos.

Harry became a little upset when he saw two large sheet-metal signs being removed from Bobbie's corner shop in his own street; the signs had greeted him every time he had been into the shop, which was almost every day of his life. No longer would he see five boys, dressed identical to himself, looking at him with happy faces, each of them eating a chocolate bar... This was being replaced by a sheet of plastic advertising 'Mars Bars'. The other sign seemed to light up the street with its bright yellow and blue colours in the form of the sun's rays. Yes... 'Brasso' metal polish was also being replaced by some unknown similar product printed out on a dour looking piece of plastic.

Harry hated plastic! He believed it was inferior to metal and something that was not permanent. This had been instilled into him from his experience with 'Bakelite' toys during the wartime years. He had always had a fascination with tin boxes, ever since going into Uncle Jack's shed as a small boy and he had built up a collection of them for himself, in which he kept his cigarette cards and marbles. But even this was now under threat.

A neighbour had handed him an empty tin which had originally contained tablets made by the popular night-time drink makers 'Horlicks'. The empty tins were quite popular with working-class male smokers – of which there were plenty. An empty Horlicks tin would house ten cigarettes and fit neatly into a waistcoat pocket and, in Harry's case, would hold fifty cigarette cards, quite safely tucked into his pocket to be swapped or shown among his friends at school. Harry had noticed these handy little tins and others like them, began to feel lighter and less robust. His suspicions were confirmed when he put one to the test by squeezing it in his hand until it crumpled. He soon learned that many tins and containers were now being made from pressed aluminium; it was much lighter than pressed steel and was considered to be the metal of the future.

He refused to accept any of these 'new fangled' aluminium tins into his collection, considering them to be not much better than the dreaded plastic. If this was the future, then he wanted none of it! At least as far as tins were concerned.

Time sped on and 1954 dawned. It was the start of a rundown of some great institutions; the CO-OP and the cinema being among the first to suffer the effects of changing trends. The CO-OP had become the biggest retailer of food and household goods throughout the nation, but its managers had rested on their laurels in the belief that the movement was so well-established they had a job for life. This had been quite true for the previous eighty years, but was now coming to an end. The Hindsford and Atherton CO-OP made an announcement that it was going to reduce the number of horses it used and replace them with motor vehicles. This resulted in a number of employees losing their jobs and the closure of one or two shops which were now facing competition from some larger than average food outlets called *supermarkets*.

The film industry started to feel the pinch, as cinema audiences began to dwindle for the first time in living memory; it reacted by producing epic films, many of them on biblical themes, shown to audiences on wide screens called 'cinemascope'; but it had little effect and it would be many years later before cinema would regain its popularity. Perhaps the greatest institution of them all was about to undergo a change from which it would never recover... Steam locomotives which had reigned supreme for more than a hundred years began to be phased out in favour of Diesel locomotives. There would be no bright future for the diesels, just acceptance in a limited form, as thousands of miles of tracks on which their predecessors had run, would also be phased out at the end of the decade.

As regards Harry's future, it was already mapped out for him by his father; he was to start an apprenticeship in the local ironworks immediately he finished school. As the eldest of five children born into a working class family, there was little incentive to stay on at school for further education. Due to lack of money, the emphasis was on leaving school, getting a job and starting to earn money. Job satisfaction or a career did not enter into the situation.

As 1954 ploughed on, the Hudsons continued their hum-drum lifestyle in their simple two up and two down house. The family rows continued as the lack of suitable accommodation began to affect them all.

Simple tasks like having a wash or bath were becoming an embarrassment among them and had to be carried out when other members of the family were out or had retired to bed. Kitty began to think of the future as she watched her children growing up very fast... it was as if the world was passing them by...

WHAT GOES AROUND, COMES AROUND...

In the Spring of 1954, Harry prepared himself for his final weeks at school. Like most boys of his age, he was not over-enthusiastic about school and looked forward to leaving, in the mistaken belief life would not be as strict and regimented. Fifteen years of a person's life was quite enough under such conditions; freedom was on the horizon; and payment for your labours (once you had started work). These were the uppermost thoughts of the working classes.

Harry sensed the first shackles of freedom were being removed when Mr Corlish informed pupils who were leaving school, they would be allowed to continue woodwork on their own initiative, during break times. He grasped this offer and felt much more confident about finishing a cigarette box to a much higher standard than he would otherwise have done under the beady eyes of that teacher. Mr Corlish had a habit of sitting at his desk and staring at each pupil for a few minutes, as they struggled to plane their wood square, before running out of the given measurements. He could tell by the worried look on a boy's face and the shaky movement of the plane or saw, that the pupil was in danger of ruining whatever he was making.

Mr Corlish's response was, "Stop work, laddie; and bring your wood to my bench."

The pupil would then carry his wood, red faced and place it on a workbench which Mr Corlish had allotted for himself. Mr Corlish would stop the rest of the class from working while he highlighted 'the stupid boy's mistake'. It was embarrassing and shaming, undermining the pupil's confidence even further. He would then pick up a plane and, in the space of a few minutes, correct the faulty piece of wood and advance it to a stage which would have taken the pupil quite a few lessons to accomplish. Harry had experienced this ordeal and was glad it no longer applied to him. It was now his intention to surprise Mr Corlish with his abilities.

Back at home, Kitty had learned that Uncle Jack's house was about to become vacant again. There was gossip in the village that the occupant of No 31, a milk round man employed by the CO-OP, was about to be dismissed and evicted from his house for contravening their rules. Kitty was rather surprised at first but, as she was on friendly terms with her neighbour at No. 31, decided it was none of her business and decided not to persue the matter until her neighbour had moved on. This came sooner rather than later; it was then Kitty made enquiries into the possibility of securing the tenancy. She was bitterly disappointed to learn that the house had been let, once again, to a CO-OP employee.

She soon became friends with her new neighbours and learned they had been offered the tenancy of No. 31 for a limited period only, after which they would have the option of buying the property.

The CO-OP was ringing the changes in the face of competition and had begun to sell off some of its assets and close two of its shops. Kitty did not know whether this was good or bad news, regarding he sale of Uncle Jack's house. It seemed obvious the tenancy would always go to an employee, yet she had always lived in hope that this might change - but buying a house was beyond her wildest dreams. There was not even the slightest possibility of them raising a deposit on a house; it was difficult enough just to make ends meet.

As usual she carried on as best as she could, making a few changes here and there which all helped to improve her family's lifestyle. She was encouraged by the thought that she would soon have a worker contributing to the family budget.

The weeks passed by rapidly and the pace of life quickened as the whole country began to enjoy the benefits of an ever increasing range of goods now becoming available to them. Monday was no longer the traditional day on which the family washing was done; this could now be varied to whenever the owner of a washing machine wished. Refrigerators began to appear on the scene in a few households; this meant certain perishable foods could be stored leading to less trips to the shops, and more time saved to spend elsewhere.

Better communication enabled people to see what news and events were going on in other parts of the country, within a few hours of them taking place via the one B.B.C. channel available to them. Telephones, however, were still considered to be an instrument of the privileged few and were only used for business – or emergencies. Apart from two public call boxes, the village of

Hindsford possessed only three private telephones in 1954; these belonged to the CO-OP, the Doctor and a local businessman. 'Radio-grams' began to replace wind-up gramophones, as radio manufacturers combined the two; it was a clever way of selling radios, which were now under threat from television. Within the space of a few years, the sales of 'Radio-grams' would take off -due to the new craze of 'pop music', from such artists as 'Bill Halley and the Comets', 'Elvis Presley', 'Slim Whitman' and 'The Beatles'. It was debatable whether any of these artists could actually sing... but that did not matter! This is what the public wanted and this is what they got. Pop stars had now become the number one icons of the younger generation, who bought millions of their records, thus ousting sportsmen and film stars from the fame they had enjoyed for many years.

At the beginning of June 1954, Harry concentrated very hard on what would be his final exams before he left school. He and his classmates had been told that, although their exam results would make no difference to them being promoted or relegated, comments on their performance would he made in their final school report. This could be a worrying situation for those who were thinking of going into a non-manual job, such as office work or journalism... In reality, this was very rare, especially for secondary school leavers seeking employment in the industrial North. Most white collar workers usually had a Grammar School education, or had attended night classes after a secondary education, or had gained promotion from the shop floor. However, since it was a period of full-time employment, there was little point in worrying too much about it. Most school leavers walked straight into a job. Most of these people did not have to produce any paperwork of their qualifications; their future employment was decided on the whim of a foreman or supervisor after a ten minute interview.

In his final week at school, Harry had been told by a couple of teachers that he was capable of much improvement. He was encouraged by this and put all his remaining school break times into finishing the cigarette box and awaiting Mr Corlish's comments. With only one day left in the school term, he presented the finished cigarette box to Mr Corlish, who had promised to insert the hinges for him, if or when Harry was finished.

"Well, well, well... I would never have believed it Hudson... I am amazed to the point of being speechless."

A few moments silence followed, Harry became a little concerned as to what Mr Corlish was *really* thinking and whether he was about to throw it in the waste bin and give him a final degrading lecture.

Finally, the silence was broken by the teacher. "Now then Hudson... Go and get two hinges from the ironmongers on the main street – and mind the traffic."

"How much will steel hinges be?"

"Steel hinges? What are you talking about laddie? The box is of sufficient quality to warrant brass hinges."

"But sir. You told me last week you would fit steel hinges and they would cost no more than sixpence - which is all I have on me..."

Mr Corlish reached into his waistcoat pocket and handed Harry a brass threepence and a penny. "There you are laddie, you've now got tenpence, which is what two brass hinges will cost. Steel hinges indeed..." he muttered.

Harry came back with the hinges and Mr Corlish told the remaining pupils to stop work and gather around his bench. This time there was no humiliation or degrading lecture; he told them to watch closely while he put the finishing touches to an extremely fine piece of work by Hudson.

Harry felt very proud at being singled out like this, it was only the third time in all his years at school that he had been commended for his efforts.

Mr Corlish then handed the box back to him and shook everyone's hand. He told them all to go out into the world and earn their living by doing the best they could.

The last day at school passed fairly quickly for those who were leaving. They were just required to tidy their desks and listen to informal chats from teachers reminiscing about the past four years they had spent with each other. Finally, at 4 P.M., school was dismissed and Harry and his classmates were free. Broad smiles came over their faces and a sense of freedom came over them as they trudged through the classroom door, held open by Mr Hall, an eccentric music teacher who handed each pupil a leaving certificate with his remaining hand; it was an un-ceremonial end to a way of life that had seemed an eternity to each one of them. Yet assuming each pupil had started school at the age of four, it was just eleven years... The following years would pass much faster...

On leaving school, Harry spent the next few weeks re-organising Uncle Jack's poultry pen which he had inherited. He could not begin work until he reached his fifteenth birthday in August, so he busied himself by re-building a couple of sheds using Uncle Jacks old tools and the new found confidence he had gained in school woodwork classes.

It was during this period that Kitty began to make further changes at home; getting rid of the old fashioned furniture they were still using. She had managed to persuade Dick that there was no point in having a new modern tiled fireplace if it was surrounded by a room full of Victorian furniture. Dick did not entirely agree and drew the line at parting with the 1930's dining table and his beloved radio.

An agreement was reached and three quarters of the family furniture was now on the condemned list. Harry spent the best part of two days dismantling the massive ornate carved Victorian sideboard and the walnut piano and turning them into firewood. Two oak fireside chairs and an Edwardian mahogany plant stand met the same fate. The Victorian lithographs, which had hung above the old mantelpiece had been removed when the new fireplace was installed and were now consigned to the dustbin. Dick suggested the whole operation was pointless and could have been put off until bonfire night. But Kitty was having none of it. She had had enough of putting things off; she was now in the business of getting things done.

Surprisingly, Dick offered little resistance, probably because there was very little mention of moving into a council house while all this was going on.

"While you're at it, you can also take down the shelf and curtain on the chimney breast wall; we'll get rid of that too." Kitty added.

"But what are we going to do with the Staffordshire pot dogs on the shelf?" Harry enquired.

"I've given them to the insurance man's wife. He was always going on about her wanting a pair of ornaments like them – so now she's got them."

Yes. Kitty was in full swing; she was making changes... and nothing, or no-one was going to stop her!

Harry began his employment in the Ironworks a few days after his fifteenth birthday in August 1954. For the first few weeks, working life seemed quite enjoyable and much better than school life. Being the youngest apprentice meant he had to do the work's errands which consisted of buying lunches, newspapers and cigarettes. He was allowed about two hours each day out of work to do this, which was a welcome break from having to spend the whole day inside the works. His experience with running old Mrs Timperley's errands enabled him to purchase the more popular brands of cigarettes which were still quite scarce, with less trouble than his predecessors had. In fact, he could usually find time for a visit to the poultry allotment to gather a few eggs and see how his little enterprise was getting on.

Harry's four pounds weekly wage was also helping to make life a little better at home. Kitty had replaced the old fashioned furniture with 'New Style' modern furniture, thanks to hire purchase agreements which did not require her husband's signature and were paid for with her new found income. There was even some talk of buying a washing machine and a television set, but it would be quite a while yet before these latest luxury items could be acquired.

Time sped on very quickly as the decade passed its half way mark. Harry was no longer the errand boy at work and Kitty now had another worker supplementing the family income. The whole nation was enjoying a period of prosperity and optimism.

In 1957 Harold Macmillan became Prime Minister and told the nation they 'had never had it so good'. This was certainly true in Harry's case, as he experienced his first holiday away from home. For the princely sum of seven pounds each, he and a few friends enjoyed a wonderful week at a boarding house above a row of shops in Blackpool.

The holiday came complete with three meals a day and shared use of a bathroom – shared between everyone in the house. The landlady herself lived up to the formidable reputation of a Blackpool landlady.

She unlocked the door to them shortly after midnight on one occasion. "What time do you call this? I suppose you have all been drinking," she scolded.

All of them meekly apologised for the inconvenience, as she blocked the threshold, looking quite fearsome in her cotton nightie, dressing gown and hair curlers. After a few minutes of 'tongue lashing', they were all allowed in and secretly given a key at breakfast time by her husband as he whispered: "Boys will be boys…"

It was a wonderful experience for all of them and a sense of achievement of having left the village for more than a day for the first time in their lives.

The Hudson family lifestyle continued to improve and by the end of 1957 they had acquired a television set and an electric washing machine. However, they still lacked the basic facility of a bathroom, which was something of a problem for the female members of the family. It was less of a problem for Harry and his father, who now had the benefit of a hot shower bath provided by their employer at the ironworks. Greatly improved social conditions towards the end of the decade led to the traditional terraced house being given a council grant of £155 towards the cost of a bathroom. It was a considerable sum of money which enabled thousands of terraced home dwellers in villages throughout the North to indulge in this sheer luxury of a private bath. The Hudsons were disappointed to learn their own application had been turned down on the grounds of insufficient room for a two up, two down to accommodate a bathroom for a family of seven. This led to frustration and further rows. Kitty once again put pressure on Harry and his father in an effort to get the whole family to move out of the village and into a council house. Yet somehow they all stayed together, arguing among themselves until the end of the decade.

In 1960, the village CO-OP began to make further cutbacks and reduced the number of employees. Among the casualties, were the Hudson's neighbours in number 31, who now owned the property.

At long last, it seemed Kitty's wish was about to come true when she learned they were moving to Blackpool and the house was to be put up for sale and also that she and her family would be given the first option to buy it!

Dick was a bit shocked when he learned the purchase price of Uncle Jack's old house was £800.

"Eight hundred bloody pounds! John Willie was offered all the houses in the row in 1931 for that money!" he griped.

This was quite true. Uncle Jack had been offered all four houses by the CO-OP for £800. As a colliery fireman and a member of staff he had been earning enough money to be able to afford it too. But that was in 1931, at the height of the economic depression when nobody's job was safe.

"It's a pity he didn't buy these houses. If he had done, then we would be calling the bloody shots, and going around with the rent book," he moaned.

He was even more shocked when he learned they would need £200 deposit, of which he and Harry would be the main contributors. He came to terms with this when a letter arrived the following day, informing Kitty of the address of a brand new council house they had been allotted outside the village.

Both he and Harry were now in a bit of a panic regarding their future abode. Dick moaned he was too old to move anywhere and Harry was adamant he was not going to move onto a council estate where everything looked the same.

"Then do something about it...and be quick or we will finish up going nowhere," shouted Kitty.

"Well I'm not going into a bloody council house and that's that!" Dick shouted back. He then retired upstairs.

When he came back down, he was clutching a handful of crisp, new five pound notes. "There! There's a hundred pounds here of bloody hard-earned cash! That's my share of a deposit on number 31."

Harry was 'gobsmacked'! Where had his father managed to get a hundred pounds from? He regained his composure when he suddenly realised that Uncle Jack's chronograph pocket watch had never been accounted for in his personal effects. He quickly put two and two together when he remembered one of his father's sayings...'you've got to live off your wits in this world'.

He decided to do likewise... "I can't match that sum of money, I don't come on to full wages until I'm twenty one and out of my apprenticeship."

"Well maybe you would be able to if you didn't go jaunting off to places like Blackpool and spending your money in the pub," said Dick.

Harry felt this was a little harsh, but said nothing as he watched his father go back upstairs, presumably to his wardrobe where he kept a biscuit tin and obviously hid his savings. This time, he came back down and threw fifty pounds onto the table. Harry decided he had no alternative but to raise the remaining fifty pounds – even if it meant not going out for a while.

The deposit was raised and a mortgage of £600 was granted to Harry and Kitty by the local council. It did not go down too well with Dick, who had provided the bulk of the deposit, when he was told he was 'too old to enter into such matters'.

The Hudsons finally moved into number 31 in October 1961. It was a dream come true and Kitty was ecstatic. For several days, she kept reciting 'It all comes to those who wait' and 'what goes around, comes around'.

Harry spent four happy years in number 31, during which time he met his future wife Margaret. They married in 1965 and moved into a house half a mile from the village and started their own family. Dick lived out his life at the house and the rest of the family all got married from the house.

In 1975, the local authorities decided to demolish most of the terraced houses in the village and replace them with modern 'semis'. Under a compulsory purchase order, a fixed sum of £800 was given to the owner of each house – regardless of its age or condition. Most of the houses had been built between 1850 and 1890 and had been landlord owned, but by this time, landlords had gone out of fashion having acquired a bad name. Most of the houses were now owned by the former tenants who had turned them into little palaces complete with bathrooms and central heating. Some of them used their £800 compensation towards purchasing another house outside the village, having been accustomed to being house owners, they did not want to go back to renting a house.

Some liked the village so much they were prepared to reverse their ownership status and go hack to renting one of the new council owned semis. As luck would have it, even they would once again become property owners under a government act carried out a few years later.

Uncle Jack's old house had served its purpose as far as the Hudsons were now concerned, especially since Kitty was the only occupant and finding the house too large to manage. However, they were not prepared to accept £800 for a house that was much larger and better built than most of the other houses. Council officials eventually agreed that number 31 and the other three adjoining houses which they referred to as the 'old CO-OP houses', were of superior construction and they increased their purchase order to £1200 per house.

This was accepted and number 31 and the rest of the row were demolished. Kitty moved into a purpose-built flat alongside many of her old neighbours and spent the rest of her life happy and content with her memories of life at number 31.

This story moves forward to the year 1999 and the Hudson family can still all be found living within a mile of the village they were born in. The village is still alive and well and, although it has retained its street names, it now lacks the character and charm of those early years.

A few of the old terraced houses managed to escape the demolition man and these houses now command high prices and are seen to be fashionable places to live.

Harry has taken early retirement from a lifetime of hard work in the iron industry; his own children have flown the nest and he is now enjoying what he likes doing best – living in the past.

His love of old furniture and bygones gave him the necessary experience to buy, sell or repair them and he is happy and content to retreat to the garden shed and wallow in the past as he fixes the legs of a Victorian chair or strips and re-polishes an old cabinet.

It is just an old hobby which he has all the time in the world to do and it earns him a bit of extra money which he spends on other old objects.

When he is indoors, he reads about such things or carefully selects a television programme that deals with the past.

Whilst he enjoys some ,modern facilities, such as central heating, a car and holidays abroad, he still goes on about modern life being 'rubbish' compared to when he was a boy. Supermarkets, mobile telephones, out of town shopping centres and TV celebrity shows would all be banned if he had his way!

His wife, Margaret's reply, is always the same: "You have too much to say my lad. You are always going on about the past and wishing you knew then, what you know now. You are still going on about that teapot you inherited from your parents… forget it and let the past go."

Harry was often rebuked for his fixation with the past and did not want to be reminded of what had happened to the only item left by his parents which had been of greater value than anything that had been left by Uncle Jack.

The teapot in question was of course, the one given to his father Dick, on the occasion of his first marriage in 1915. It had suffered the same fate as some of the other items from the Hudson household — broken by children; only this time the children were Harry's own. The loss of a family heirloom is bad enough, but when he had learned it was a fine rare piece of 'Regency' pottery, worth several hundred pounds, he had found it very hard to forget.

On a fine June afternoon in 2003, Harry was sitting in his greenhouse enjoying a pipe full of tobacco, whilst basking in the sun's warm rays. As usual, he was reminiscing and realised it was exactly fifty years to the day since his father had sold off the contents of Uncle Jack's house.

The pipe fell from his mouth as he drifted into a sleep, which usually lasted about half an hour. Margaret considered it to be his afternoon nap and rarely disturbed him because she enjoyed the quiet. On this occasion he had only been asleep for a few minutes when he was woken by her. She told him there was a van outside the front door and its owner had brought a couple of items for repair.

The visitor was told to bring the items into the garden shed and place them onto the workbench for close inspection and an estimate of the work involved. Harry rubbed the sleep from his eyes and began to survey the work. He cast his eyes over an old dining chair, which was certainly of the Regency period and noticed that the 'splat' support of the back of the chair was devoid of all its varnish. Nothing unusual about that... a chair of such age would certainly be well worn in that area. But there were other similarities about the chair which set his mind thinking; such as its woven straw seat and the unusual design of the turned legs.

The visitor returned to the shed and placed his second item on the work bench. It was a fine mahogany clock case belonging to a 'Vienna Regulator', which was a popular 19th century wall clock.

Harry closely examined the mahogany case and noticed that one of the finials was missing from the ornamental pediment.

A strange feeling came over him as he enquired where the two items had come from.

"My father bought them from a house sale about fifty years ago... They belonged to an old man called Jack Howell who lived in Green Street in Hindsford village."

For once in his life, Harry was speechless.

THE END

Printed in the United Kingdom
by Lightning Source UK Ltd.
108245UKS00001BA/8